ZERO LONELINESS

A Practical Guide to Embrace Loneliness and Transform it into Personal Empowerment and Inner Growth

RAHUL KAPOOR

“

Solitude is fine but you need someone to tell that solitude is fine.

”

HONORÉ DE BALZAC

NEED FOR THIS BOOK

IT'S A CRUEL WORLD. You want to remain isolated it will help you to the chore. You don't want to step out it will assist you in every means. We are surrounded by so much of *artificialism* nowadays, known by the name of technology and digitalisation, that the time we think about doing something for ourselves it will immediately step up, grab us from all the corners and curb our feeling of going out and meeting people. For instance, when we feel the urge to talk to someone, rather than going out to meet our friends and loved ones, we often prefer to pick up our phones and call instead. And, as soon as we put our thumb to unlock this pocket dynamite, a vast explosion of notifications pop up. The Big Bang occurred millions of years ago, but today, it's happening in everyone's daily routine. Before dialling our loved one's number, we are often intrigued by a food delivery app or a shopping platform filled with plethora of offers. If we try to ignore these distractions and move on to the dialling section, social media is ready to captivate us with its deceptive illusion of endless reels and a sea of videos. If we somehow manage to remain unperturbed by all of this (which is next to impossible) then WhatsApp, the latest news app, or any banking software will be our final stop point which will completely immerse us in its ocean of information. By this time, all our feelings of communicating with our loved ones are washed away, as if we've been placed in a washing machine, and we won't be allowed to come out until we are completely dry.

We have 8 million people around us. Yes, you cannot see and meet them all at once, but we all have the same opportunity to connect with each other, just like they do. But, still we feel *lonely*. Why is it that, despite everything and everyone around us, we still feel parched and isolated? Let me be honest. We all long for social connections. We all love to meet others, speak our heart out and express our feelings. Even if someone disagrees with me, claiming they don't crave meeting people, deep down they still carry that unfulfilled desire to empathize and be understood. We all have a very profound historical background and this is proved in our evolutionary evidence. Our ancestors, thousands of years ago, fought for survival against harsh climates and predators. But over the course of evolution, they discovered that the greatest challenge wasn't the environment or wild animals—it was *isolation*. Roaming alone, hunting alone, and remaining isolated became the major root causes of their life's obstacles. Once they realized this, they began meeting with fellow comrades and devised new survival strategies—creating tools for hunting, hunting in groups, living together as tribes, and forming social connections. They discerned that this was the only way to live long, but sadly, in this era of supercomputers and artificial intelligence, we have forgotten that path altogether, becoming completely distracted from what truly brings happiness and survival. Thank God, we still have the learnings and wisdom of early man, and the vast history of our evolution will continue to guide us on this journey from loneliness to prosperity.

When I was writing on this never ending subject of loneliness then few questions popped up in my mind.

Why do we need to learn about loneliness when we are already overwhelmed by it?

Do we actually need to be alone?

Who am I to tell anyone about this?

Well, that's right. I'm no one to tell anyone how to live their life. As for my introduction, I'm just a simple person who once struggled with the disease of loneliness, feeling as if I was controlled by both internal and external forces. I was more thinking about the outer world rather than listening to my inner voices. Overthinking was my daily routine and anxiety, anger and fear controlled my days with their firm grip. This book is a reflection of my personal experiences and how I managed to emerge from that dreaded world of seclusion, where it feels as if no one belongs to you. Even you don't feel yourself. You feel lost and like you will never be found. But don't worry, if an ordinary person like me can overcome this, then you, my friend, will surely emerge from it with flying colours. Just stay connected with me throughout this book, and by the end of it, you will feel much braver and happier. I promise.

We are surrounded by so many mixtures – air is a mixture, water is a mixture and our food is also a mixture. This leads us to believe that everything is meant to be mixed, which is why we often mix up loneliness with aloneness. If we ask people about the difference between loneliness and aloneness, 99% would say they are the same. But no, my friend, there is a huge difference—not just a minor one. This book will help you understand the contrasts between these intermingled concepts in a precise and clear manner.

So, are you ready to break free from the illusion of loneliness and illuminate your path of glory by embracing aloneness?

Great! Let's move ahead.

To

All the busy people,

Who feel lonely inside.

CONTENTS

INTRODUCTION

IN THIS HUMAN RACE, everyone is the same. By 'same', I am not referring to external appearances or social status, but to one major internal factor. And that is, *love for self.* We all love ourselves. I may sound cynical here, but this is the truth. Whenever we see a group photograph, we look for ourselves first. Whenever we hear our name in a crowd, we immediately stop and look back, even if someone else was called with a similar name. At any award function, when we see many shields and trophies, we always try to find where our name is among them. These little yet very critical hints suggest that we love ourselves more than anyone else in this world. Well, there's nothing wrong with loving oneself, but the bigger question lies in how we express this love for ourselves. Confused? Let me elaborate.

We all have aspirations, dreams, and desires to become something in life—whether it's our ambitions or the superheroes of our dreams. But how many of us actually break free from those dreams and start working on them in reality? I know your answer, and I can see you smiling. See? It's proven once again that we are all the same. We know that we love ourselves, but what we need to learn and develop is how to express that love for ourselves. This love for self is self-esteem and expression of that love is self-respect. We all have loads of self-esteem, but when it comes to self-respect, we often struggle to fulfil that. Another intermingled concept but with distinct meanings.

I always wanted to become a cricketer and play for my country. My idol was Sachin Tendulkar. Why? Ask any '90s kid and it will take hydraulic brakes to stop them from praising Sachin. It was not only the batting techniques of the Little Master but also his intriguing smile and the modesty with which he played that graced the game of cricket. Let's come back to the point. I was a good batsman (and I'm not boasting). I truly was. However, that dream remained just a dream because I never pursued it diligently and religiously. Many of my friends urged me to go to the stadium for practice and take my cricketing career seriously, but I found more satisfaction and happiness in my dreams than in reality. The consequence? You guessed it right. I was not able to play for my country. Although I was talented, that talent needed to be backed up by passion and hard work, and there I failed to do so. So, I had a lot of self-esteem, but I showed very little self-respect to myself. This literally broke me inside, and I began to feel anxious and lonely because I didn't know what else to do. I didn't have a plan B (well, I never really had a plan A either). It's not just me, there are millions of people who long to become something in life but somehow can't achieve it, living their lives forever in regret and wistfulness. This book is specifically designed for all my friends to help them come out of this wistfulness and move towards hopefulness and cheerfulness.

Seclusion and solitude have one major aspect that distinguishes them - *voluntariness.* Everything in life revolves around this word, and it further differentiates between successful and unsuccessful people. What is voluntary? It simply means something done with complete awareness and mindfulness. If we are fully aware of what we are doing and our minds are entirely focused in the right direction, then even the Almighty helps us in our endeavours. Otherwise, we only look for excuses and places to hide, which ultimately leads to loneliness. One feels isolated because they are unaware of their thoughts and actions. The energy they are expending is directed entirely in the wrong direction, which is why they are not producing the desired results. On the other hand, mindfulness and awareness can help an individual navigate through difficult situations and realign them with their goals and desires. We will discuss this awareness throughout the book and *together* devise methods to overcome the fear and anxiety associated with isolation. In short, this book revolves around one word: voluntary.

ROOT CAUSES

YUVAL NOAH HARARI in his epic book *Sapiens – A Brief History of Humankind* depicted how early man fought hard for its survival, constantly moving from place to place in search of food and forming social bonds with other human groups. They strived to make connections but when they saw any sapiens becoming burden to their tribe they either left them behind or killed them. So, whenever we feel left behind or neglected by our group, we often experience anxiety and fear. We get the sense that our survival is at risk. This feeling is known as loneliness. I hope that whenever you feel isolated now, you'll start connecting it to your ancestral past. The reason we feel isolated lies in our evolution. Though thousands of years have passed, our minds remain wired this way. Strange but true.

Experiences play a major role in shaping our perspective toward anything and anyone. If our experiences are positive, our outlook will be favourable, and bad otherwise. So not only our ancestral past but our childhood also is greatly influenced by this one word, which further affects our overall attitude toward life. Since childhood, I have witnessed my mother struggling with physical pain (I have mentioned this numerous times in my previous books because it has profoundly impacted my childhood and contributed to my feelings of loneliness and stress). She suffered from rheumatoid arthritis early in her life, and until her last breath, we witnessed her crying in excruciating pain. This childhood experience of witnessing my mother in such agony filled me with anger and hatred. Hatred toward certain relatives who, in that situation, never helped us and, in fact, seemed pleased to see us in such a dire state. Whenever I saw my friends' mothers walking properly and smiling, I asked myself why my mother was unable to walk and always crying. These are life's ways of teaching and making people stronger and better, but how can this be explained to a child under 10 years old? I was clueless, and this experience made me bitter inside, leading me to distance myself from others. I know I am not alone in this. There are thousands of children like me who, due to their bitter experiences, develop a strong dislike for people and life, making it take years to overcome those feelings. Some, due to their parents' bad behaviour, build resentment toward them, while others face various forms of mental or physical harassment from people, friends, or even relatives, which contributes to their loneliness. Some children witness their parents quarrelling all the time and may even see one parent leave the other in extreme scenarios. Overall, childhood experiences play a major role in shaping our behaviour toward life and others.

All the above childhood scenarios contribute to mental agony, but what about physical pain? There are people who suffer from diseases and illnesses from birth or very early in life. This is not their fault, yet they often feel inferior, leading to feelings of isolation. Here again, negative experiences with people give rise to resentments and grudges. If someone is born with *special needs,* then mostly these near-and-dear ones, close relatives, friends and even neighbours, mock them and express pitifulness. I have expressed my own anger, but I also wonder how my mother must have felt lying in bed throughout her life. How must she would have felt seeing the world walking around and working normally while she could only move in a wheelchair? These experiences are incredibly cruel and can fill anyone's heart with deep bitterness and hostility. But don't worry; where there is a problem, a solution often lies nearby. Read on, and we will explore the solutions in the upcoming sections.

As I mentioned earlier, this is a cruel world. It speaks of all the good and rosy things but simultaneously expects you to perform all your duties perfectly and, most importantly, alone. It is always quick to take credit for your work, but if you make a mistake, it will be the first to turn away.

Modern society always emphasizes doing things alone. Although we see many quotes on social media and in our daily lives about teamwork and synchronization, the truth is that everyone is on their own in this highly competitive world. To make matters worse, technology plays a significant role in exacerbating this situation. We are all caged in our small pocket devices, and this technology is further driving us to become even lonelier. This illustrates how alone we are in this highly populated world and it's not a choice but extremely imperative that we learn how to survive and transform this loneliness into aloneness.

Are you up for the challenge?

THE IMPACT.......

HUMAN LIFE PASSES THROUGH various cycles from birth to death—childhood, adolescence, adulthood, and old age. We learned this in biology, where the transition was illustrated, showing a sweet, innocent child growing into a frail, elderly man. But who can explain these stages to loneliness? No one. That's why it affects us at each stage of our life and sometimes very adversely affects it. A small immature child can feel alone, just as a fully mature individual experiences the same emotion. One thing we must acknowledge about loneliness is that it isn't biased. It treats everyone equally, affecting all in the same way. Everyone in the grip of loneliness feels isolated, though the reason for that isolation differs at each stage of life. It is this underlying reason—the logic behind the loneliness—that impacts us differently through the various cycles of our existence. For instance, a child may feel lonely if they are bullied at school because of their physical appearance or struggle to make friends after moving to a new city with their parents. A teenager might feel lonely because of unique interests they've developed, especially if they can't find a supportive group of friends in college. A young individual might feel isolated when facing early challenges at work or struggling with sexual performance in their relationship. Similarly, an older individual might feel anxious at the thought of spending the rest of their life alone after the death of their partner or because their children have left them feeling abandoned. There can be many reasons for loneliness, but understanding these factors can help us grasp its impact more deeply. Let's explore further.

The most common form of loneliness is emotional isolation. In fact, many adults around the world struggle with this type of loneliness significantly. When we were children, we always wanted to grow up quickly to fulfil our dreams and aspirations. We believed life would be amazing as adults, with no one telling us what to do or what not to do. We imagined we could pursue whatever we wanted and desired. What a mirage that was! Isn't it? When we grew up, we all wished we could go back to our childhood because the reality turned out to be quite different. There were more rules and instructions from the world, and whenever we tried to follow our own path, we often found ourselves feeling alone. Even our partners. Very seldom do we find understanding partners in this selfish world, instead, most of us feel deprived of such connections and continue to struggle with emotional isolation. Consequence – it leads to high anxiety, depression and unwanted stress. This type of loneliness stems from our internal environment but apart from this there is another type where we crave for social network or group of friends with whom we could interact and fulfil our social needs. We could chat, gossip, or discuss our problems with friends, but often, due to factors like personality traits, lack of shared interests, not knowing anyone properly or being new to a particular place, we end up falling victim to social loneliness.

Another type of loneliness is triggered by our philosophical thoughts, where we feel isolated in a world filled with people. As we wander through our inner thoughts, we often question our purpose and existence on this planet. This type of loneliness is often experienced by individuals who have achieved success or hold a prominent position in life, yet they still feel a sense of hollowness and an urge to fill that emptiness inside. We have seen many such examples of people who, at the peak of their careers, surprise everyone by deciding to leave it all behind in search of peace and freedom.

Adding to this type of isolation is intellectual loneliness, where a person grapples with unique thoughts and ideas that are unlike anything else. They often feel that they have no one to share these ideas with because they believe very few people will understand them, or they worry that their thoughts might become a laughingstock among their peers. Regardless of the type, they all overlap to some extent, and they stem from a common source: a lack of courage and confidence. One common thread runs through all forms of isolation, which is the feeling of disconnection. Addressing this feeling of disconnection is extremely important. Without doing so, one might feel suffocated inside and could even succumb to their loneliness. Let's move forward and get ready to tackle this loneliness, welcoming the moments of aloneness in our lives.

BEFORE WE PROCEED...

TILL NOW I HAVE DISCUSSED a lot about loneliness and aloneness but it would be a big mistake on my part if I don't clarify these concepts before moving forward. While they may seem like identical twins, they possess different natures and characteristics, much like twin children. So, here we go.

Everything revolves around mind-set and so do we. We tend to do whatever our mind-set is telling us to do. Therefore, our perspective plays a crucial role in either separating us from ourselves or bringing us together. When we are unaware of the situations and surroundings around us, completely lost in our internal world without any meaning or purpose, and neglecting the signals our body and mind send us, we tend to fall into a state known as loneliness. Whatever we do, be it, driving, cooking, working and even sleeping, we often get lost in a flood of thoughts and become completely submerged in a sea of overthinking. We feel deprived of everything in life and feel as if we are not needed in this world. We don't put our heart into our work because our minds are wandering elsewhere, lost in our thoughts. We feel as though nobody loves us and that we are unlikable. In this state, we become overly dependent on the external world, valuing others' opinions more than our own. This occurs because we don't feel empowered enough. We doubt ourselves at every step of our life and love to follow what others are doing. This is why many engineers end up working in the banking and insurance sectors. They overlook their true talents and instead follow the advice of their parents, society, cousins, and neighbours. They make this decision because they lack inner empowerment and have not been made aware of their true potential. This should have been addressed at the school level. The real reason a child is sent to school is to become aware of their true talents and potential, enabling them to pursue their dreams and aspirations. Unfortunately, the entire academic system revolves around marks and grades. Pictures of students with high grades are displayed in the reception area to encourage others to follow in their footsteps. Following is not inherently wrong, but it shouldn't be done blindly. One should draw inspiration from top performers to excel in their own fields, rather than trying to succeed in areas for which they are not suited. You cannot ask a fish to climb a tree, yet unfortunately, everyone is measured by the same yardstick and this failure to recognize individual potential can lead to feelings of loneliness.

But don't worry. There is a simple and straightforward solution that can empower anyone to discover their true self. It involves transforming loneliness into aloneness or seclusion into solitude. Though it may sound difficult, trust me, it is not. Once you take the first step, it becomes easier. It's a process involving a few steps in the right direction that can lead you from adversity to prosperity. So, what is aloneness? In simple terms, it's a form of loneliness, but one that is voluntary. It means we choose to be alone. But you might be saying, 'Rahul, how can anyone choose to be alone when loneliness feels so toxic?' Well, that's the beauty of our mind-set. Once it aligns in the right direction, it fills with positive thoughts, making everything around us seem adorable and beautiful. That can only happen if we start loving ourselves, respecting ourselves, removing every iota of doubt from our minds and finding our real purpose in life. I am again saying, it's not at all difficult. I can stamp this from my personal experience. It's just like putting a derailed train back on track and at the same time fixing and clearing the track ahead so that it doesn't get derailed again.

Aloneness is simply loving yourself, admiring yourself, and most importantly accepting yourself the way you are. You are not meant to imitate others, right? You are sent on this planet with some predefined motive but many people keep following others and go back without fulfilling their real purpose. Aloneness is fun as you can get ample time to work on your dreams and aspirations. You will not be cursing yourself as you are not following anyone's instructions but your own. You will be happily working on enhancing your skills and upgrading your talents which will further transcend you to the real success. So, without further ado, let's jump straight to the first step that will eliminate all your worries and take you on a wonderful journey from seclusion to solitude.

Are you ready my friend?

PART I.
Preparation

1.
HIT THE DELETE BUTTON

WE USE THIS BUTTON quite often in our daily lives but very seldom we realise that we could utilise the same button in our personal lives too, to release a lot of distress and worry. It's a popular cliché that *the mind replays what heart can't delete* and it holds a lot of significance in this first step toward adopting aloneness. And, this replay converts our thinking into overthinking. When a particular thought keeps revolving in our minds like a never ending loop it creates that unwanted stress and anxiety. Hitting the delete button is nothing but deleting unnecessary things, habits and even, people from our lives. You must be wondering why have I started with this negative point. Why deletion is the first step? Well the logic is pretty simple. Suppose you are shifting to a new house and it is all cluttered. Everything is haywire from doors to walls to wooden stuff to garden and even washrooms. Will you be able to breathe properly in such a place? Will you be able to live happily there? No. Pure thoughts are never generated in an unorganised mind and environment. That is the reason we should delete first and then move ahead.

Deletion brings space. Deletion brings scope. A scope of adding something new. Our minds are cluttered with so much stuff be it office work, house work, expectations, ambitions, rivalries, resentments, comparisons, envy, achievements, frustrations, disappointments and on and on and on. The list is endless. If we sit down once and write everything what our mind stores, we would wonder how much pressure we put on our brain and that is the reason why we feel burnout most of the times. But, who in this digital age has the time to do this trivial task? No one. Yes, we cannot remove everything from our life but surely there are many things for which a need is created and which was never required to live a peaceful life. Stuff like digital assistants (DAs), social media overload, unworn jewellery, subscriptions and many more. What these things have done to us is created a *dependency*. We have become so much dependent on digital assistants that without them our world seems to be hopeless whereas earlier we were living a decent life without them. Why should we remove or should we say, reduce them (as without them also there is no way out)? There is very less human interaction and involvement with these digital assistants around. Earlier, we used to connect with our friends, colleagues or relatives for any kind of information or even discussions on critical issues but with DAs that interaction is reduced considerably. Not only interaction but our emotional connect is also reduced a lot with DAs around. While conversing with friends we also discussed about other matters like families, work, passions, crushes, achievements, problems and other stuff but that human touch is long gone with digitisation. This, inadvertently, has created a huge void inside us which has moved us toward isolation as for everything we tend to go to ChatGPT, Siri or Alexa. Although, this is also the need of the hour but over-exposure of these assistants has dented our social life big time and hence created loneliness.

After finishing our work, we often turn to leisure time. But how do we spend it? Most of us grab our phones and get lost in reels, shorts, and endless videos. While watching, we often start feeling hungry and end up ordering food online. Then, it hits us that the groceries need restocking, so we place that order online too. While ordering groceries, our attention often shifts to the latest offers on clothes and accessories. In the same way, we pay bills, manage subscriptions, transfer funds, enrol in educational courses, and even date—everything is done online. Huh! With so much happening online and so little human interaction, how can we not feel lonely. In the past, we used to do all these things physically, moving around and engaging with the world. Back then, if we needed groceries, we had to plan ahead, write out a list, and go to the store. We'd check every item carefully, comparing prices and features with other brands. It was a good mental workout, along with the physical effort of pushing the cart and handling the kids. But now, that all feels like too much hassle. Who gives a damn about planning, writing, moving, analysing, picking and bringing them home. Just pick up the smartphone and order in minutes. How smart these e-commerce companies are! They know everyone loves comfort and convenience, and people are willing to pay the price—even if it costs them their physical and mental health—for this coziness.

We really need to cut back on all this. I'm not against modern conveniences, but we forget to set boundaries. When we see something that looks great and beneficial, we grab onto it without thinking twice. That's why older people always say, 'Everything needs to be done in moderation.' But not many people realize this until after they've faced some sort of loss. There's no doubt that we save time with these conveniences, but how we use that saved time is just as critical. We need to figure out what digital tools we really need and what's just a product of our endless wants—things that are actually doing more harm than good. We need to genuinely cut back on these things, and over time, we'll notice a lot of positive changes in our mental state and peace of mind. This sense of serenity and calmness will help us shift from feeling lonely to embracing aloneness.

It's much easier to say than to actually do. This applies everywhere. We've talked about how reducing digital activities can really help us, but we need to make sure we put that into practice in real life. But how is this even possible with so many apps, software, and digital assistants out there, all waiting to wrap their arms around us and pull us back into that relaxation mode? The solution lies in our habits. If we develop good habits and stick to them with discipline, it won't matter whether we're in the digital age, agricultural age, or industrial age. We won't be bothered by distractions and can keep moving toward wisdom and success. Habits are nothing but our regular behaviours that are repeated consistently that they become automatic with little conscious thought or effort. Repetition is the key here and this repetitiveness has a profound impact on our overall well-being and productivity.

For example, if you make it a habit to meet friends at least once a week or attend a social event every couple of weeks, it will eventually become automatic and won't require scheduling. Similarly, if you develop an interest in a sport or hobby like table tennis, swimming, or badminton, regularly attending classes, then it will send a signal to your subconscious mind that it's time to get moving, so you won't end up sitting idle at home. We feel lonely only when we don't perform a task. In simple words, we are not doing any action and this sends wrong signals to our mind which makes us anxious and worried. I don't have to look far to prove this as I used to struggle with good habits myself. My whole day used to be spent daydreaming. Even in school, during class, I'd get lost in thoughts of playing cricket. Trust me, I'd run entire matches in my mind, complete with the toss and the final result. Dreaming isn't bad, but failing to turn those dreams into action is simply unacceptable. I used to wake up late, never exercised, and didn't focus on my goals. Overall, I wasn't going anywhere, and I paid a hefty price for it. I developed lower back pain, which caused my health to deteriorate and ultimately washed away my dream of playing cricket. This filled me with deep agony and low self-esteem, and I began to disconnect from everyone. I would isolate myself and dwell on the past. I didn't realize when this thinking turned into deep rumination, but whenever I was alone, I would find myself dwelling on the past. This went on for many years, and I felt like I was just stagnant, like still water. Then one day, I decided to change my entire attitude toward life. I resolved to change every habit that was holding me back. The first thing I did was pick up a pen and paper. I started journaling every learning or experience—good, bad, or ugly. I changed my daily routine: waking up on time, getting to the office on time, going to bed at a regular hour, and cutting down on junk food, replacing it with a healthier diet. You can probably guess the results. Yes, they've been tremendous! Everything is back on track, and now I feel much happier and more content with my work and my routine. Before, I used to criticize myself, but now I've learned to love myself. I'm making new friends and helping them out. I also don't hesitate to seek support from others when I need it, something I never did before. We often think we can do everything on our own, but that's just an old myth, like the belief that the Earth was flat. The truth is, the Earth isn't flat, and we can't handle everything on our own. At every stage of our lives, we need people to mentor, support, and guide us. Those who embrace this principle become leaders, while the rest simply follow their lead. This raises an important question: how can we develop good habits when we have so-called 'near and dear ones' ready to criticize us, pull us down, and push us back into our bad habits? You know where I'm going with this—it's time to hit the delete button on some of those people in our lives.

Jim Rohn once said, 'You are the average of the five people you spend the most time with,' and that couldn't be more true today. You really do become like the people you surround yourself with. You stay with a leader, you acquire leadership qualities. You spend time with a finisher, you develop a finishing mind-set. You spend time with result oriented people, you become efficient. And, vice versa. This vice versa holds great significance. Gossipers convert you into gossiper. Laggards turn you into a laggard. Procrastinators drag you into procrastination. So, it's important to evaluate the people around us. Who are they? What are their habits? What are their goals in life? What are their action plans? What are their achievements so far? You should always ask yourself these questions before choosing your companions. Dig deeper and ask even more questions. Be absolutely certain, because these people will *for sure* impact the direction of your life.

Now, let's talk about who these people are. 'People around you' are everyone apart from you. People often think that its only about outsiders but the insiders whom we call 'relatives' are even more venomous and, are the biggest procrastinators and draggers in life (Not all but most of them). They don't achieve much in life, and they often make sure others stay stuck in the same place too. There's a simple litmus test for identifying these people: pay attention to their words and actions. Whenever you notice a mismatch between what they say and what they do, it's best to just walk away. Keep your distance from such people, even if they're close friends or family. It doesn't matter. There's an old saying: it's better to have wise enemies than foolish friends. Because in the end, they'll either pull you down to their level or get you into a lot of trouble, and people often regret that later on. So, I humbly urge you to put everyone—and I mean *everyone*—through this litmus test. This way, they won't be able to turn your life into a reflection of their shortcomings and negativity.

Congratulations on clearing the first level of your transition from loneliness to aloneness! Now that you've removed negative thoughts, habits, and people from your life, you must be feeling pretty relaxed, relieved, and lighter. But at the same time, you might be wondering what to do next. Let's move on to the next step, where we'll use this newfound spare time to focus on developing and accepting ourselves.

Are you excited?

2.
ACCEPTANCE

Accept the truth that no matter how much you are surrounded by people, the end will always be loneliness.

NOTHING IN THIS WORLD is inherently good or bad. Everything depends on you. Your perspective. How you perceive a situation may be completely different from someone else's point of view. What seems unfavourable to you might actually benefit someone else. Acceptance means acknowledging people, circumstances, life, and most importantly, yourself, just *as they are*. We often assume that everyone thinks in the same way as we do, but this is one of life's biggest misconceptions. We expect our partners to act a certain way while they prefer to behave in some other manner. We like them in blue but they prefer wearing red. We gift our loved ones a pack of chocolates but they might be expecting a bouquet of roses. This difference in thinking and opinions often results in partners separating and becoming deeply immersed in loneliness. We think we could change the people around but this world sings and dance to its own tunes. Truth of the matter is we cannot change anything but, ourselves.

And, to change ourselves we need to accept ourselves first. If you are an old school, you should not feel ashamed but be proud of it. If you could not afford a luxurious car but a small budget car, then don't overburden yourself with higher debt just to show off. Just accept the way you are. If you have bad temper, accept it and work on changing that behaviour. Ask yourself what makes you angry most of the time - Is it the taunting of people around you? Is it bad habits? Or, Is it scarcity of money? What is it? Take a moment to sit down, relax and focus on improving your behaviour. You will find a solution for sure. However, if you expect people to embrace you and understand your bad behaviour, I'm sorry, my friend, but you are fooling yourself.

Identify the emotions tied to your loneliness that regularly push you back into your shell. Why do you feel sad? Why do you feel empty inside? What makes you fearful? We are often afraid to confront these questions because we don't want to accept reality. We prefer to stay immersed in our pool of illusions, as it makes us feel comfortable and gives us the false hope that things will change over time and that people will eventually behave the way we want them to. But this is not true. Not at all. Answering these pressing questions may be difficult at first, but this probing and searching for the 'reality behind the actual circumstances' will eventually lead you to a much better 'territory of solutions' that gradually guides you toward the truth. This truth can be very difficult to swallow at first, but once you learn the art of digesting it, trust me, you will be much better off mentally and physically. In other words, work on the root causes of your isolation. If you are feeling lonely on a regular basis what is it that is pushing you toward this persistent sense of loneliness. Are you expecting too much from others? Are you not prioritising your needs? Are you sacrificing your feelings and emotions just to make others happy? What is it? It could be due to people discarding you because of the way you speak, your height, or your heavy voice. They might even be jealous of your profound wisdom. Pay attention to these subtle cues and how people's behaviour change toward you. What is the trigger point? Once you focus closely, you will be able to identify the triggers that make you feel inferior.

Once you have identified those triggers and pressures, ask yourself about the essence of your identity. If you look, speak, walk, or do anything in this world in a certain way, that's okay. That's your unique way of doing it. No one in this world can tell you how to do it. You know why? Because your true nature will always take over. If you enjoy silence but pretend to enjoy being in a noisy place just to fit in with a group, sooner or later, you will turn away from that environment and seek solace in a more peaceful setting. It doesn't matter who says 'what' or 'how much' about you. If you love yourself, understand yourself, and accept yourself completely, then no one can dismantle your peace of mind. Nobody can make you sad, and no one will be able to hurt you.

Let me share a secret with you. This world is always hungry for leaders. Yes. And, people love to follow. Wherever we go, we see pictures of leaders, gurus and mentors painted all across the cities and nations. And, there isn't just one chief across, there are many. What does this imply? It clearly shows that despite the many leaders already present, there is always room for more chiefs. My humble question to you is: if there is so much scope for leadership in this world and people need more leaders to enlighten their wisdom, then why can't it be you? Why can't you become a mentor to others? You might be laughing and saying, 'Rahul, stop kidding.' But trust me, this is possible. The only thing you need to do is embrace yourself. If you accept yourself as you are, if you love your identity and if you work according to your innate beliefs and ethics, then there is no doubt in my mind that you can - and will - become a leader one day. Anybody can. Anyone with strong morals and pure intentions to help others can become a leader. And the great news is that one need not shout it out loud. It is their good deeds and helpful attitude toward others that will make them truly pious and sacred. Mother Teresa is a name that resonates deeply with this truth. She never boasted about her remarkable work, yet her deeds spread like an eternal fragrance, enlightening the world with peace and harmony. Why was Mother Teresa able to achieve this? Because she accepted everything about herself and the world. She had confidence in her ability to act in accordance with her ethics. She loved herself first, which allowed her to disperse that love to others. This incredible trust in herself transformed her into a world leader and an immortal soul.

We all are hard masters. A trait we have learnt from our teachers and elders. Have you ever noticed how adults speak to children or how senior officials communicate with juniors? It's always filled with instructions, lessons, and scoldings. Very seldom do we see someone in a position of authority showing kindness to those at lower levels. Sadly, we learn to treat people this way and often begin to emulate the same behaviour. But we don't stop there. We go further and treat ourselves the same way. This self-treatment becomes the biggest hindrance on our path to self-acceptance. This self-harshness often leads to our isolation, so it needs to be addressed critically yet with kindness. Unkindness stems from the fact that we often trust others more than ourselves. We tend to accept whatever the world around us tells us without applying our own wisdom. We compare ourselves too much to others, as if we are all identical offsprings. These are signs of low self-esteem and a fear of failure. The illusion of perfectionism is also a major contributor to our low self-confidence. All these factors combined deter us from believing that we can survive alone and find joy. Charity begins at home and kindness starts with self. If we treat ourselves with empathy, compassion, and gentleness, it will be reflected in our behaviour toward others and that will help strengthen our bonds, further.

In his bestselling book, *Don't Believe Everything You Think*, author Joseph Nguyen very aesthetically put forward an astonishing fact about truth. He says "If you want to find the truth, look for simplicity". He further adds that truth cannot be refined any further whereas complexities can be. A truth is true in itself. It just needs to be simple. These statements underscore the essence of acceptance. If we want to accept ourselves fully and completely, we must be true to ourselves. We need to embrace ourselves in every sense and work toward our own betterment, as well as that of the world around us. Then, there will be no space left for fear and loneliness, and we will sense profound joy.

Well done! You have successfully completed the second level. I hope you're feeling a little lighter and cooler by now. Great! This is what good preparation does: it relieves us of undesired anxiety and readies us for upcoming challenges. Let's move on to the next critical phase of this transition process, where we will dive a little deeper and apply our preparation to build a solid foundation.

Does that sound good?

PART II.
Foundation

3.
Setting the Intentions

"

Energy flows where intentions goes.

"

WHY DO YOU NEED SOLITUDE? What is actually the requirement? You are lonely either way. But, what sets the tone for aloneness (solitude) is the intentions. This intention is something, or I should say everything, that separates the loneliness from the aloneness. This reinforces the concept of 'Voluntary Solitude' we explored earlier in the book, where we consciously choose to be alone and embrace solitude. Intentions are vital for anything, even for enjoyment. Suppose we want to go out and have fun but don't know where to go? Which place to visit? Should we go to a park or a mall or a concert or a gallery? We are uncertain about it. So do you think anyone will be able to enjoy with such unclear mind-set? No one can. Intentions have three basic underlying principles without which it is just a vague desire or a fleeting thought – *Consciousness, Purpose and Internal Desire.* Allow me to explain this with an analogy.

Suppose you have decided to plant a tree but just hoping does not help your cause. You actually needed to be aware (*Consciousness*) of the place, conditions and climate for the same to flourish. Then you need to decide which type of tree you want to grow. Is it an apple tree, lemon tree, oak tree or a maple tree? This second step decides why you are planting a tree? (What is the end *purpose*?) You want fruit, wood, oil or you want to help mother earth and give something back. What is it? This second step answers all these queries. And, once you are clear with all the doubts and ambiguities, you will be all set and motivated to water it, nurture and helping it thrive. This final step of taking care (*internal desire*) will help the plant become a large fruitful tree and help you fulfil your desired objective.

Now, let's apply this understanding to the process of transitioning from loneliness to solitude.

UNDERSTAND YOUR LONELINESS

Try to gauge why you feel lonely most of the times? What is that one thing that is killing you inside and actually stopping you from expressing yourself? As I mentioned earlier, you need to ask yourself questions. In fact, as many as you can. The truth is, many of us even fear asking questions. Since childhood, we've taken so many exams, and from that experience, the fear of questions has become deeply ingrained in us. Also, whenever we asked questions as children, we were often "shut down" by our parents, teachers, or other elders. This made us so afraid of asking questions because we knew someone would likely scold us harshly. What's worse is, we don't even ask questions to ourselves— the very questions whose answers could put our lives back on track. Alas! Because of our past experiences, we hesitate to ask questions and don't move forward. But don't worry—everyone goes through that same phase of being scolded during childhood. You're not alone in this. Relax. Take a few deep breaths and gently ask your subconscious about your loneliness. This sub-consciousness is nothing but *you*. It's connected to divinity and will never scold you. Check if your loneliness is due to a lack of social connections, unmet emotional needs, past experiences, or any recent transitions in your life, such as moving to a new city or the end of a relationship or any other reason. Being conscious with yourself will help you find the right answers to your problems. Try to identify the thoughts that arise when you feel alone and how you behave during those moments. There is a pattern to everything that happens. Just try to figure that out.

Few instances of thoughts that often bother people who feel alone. *'Nobody loves me' or 'No one cares about me'*. These are common reasons for disconnecting from others, as many assume these beliefs to be true. Another thought is - *'If I open up, they will call me weird and will reject me'*. This is also an assumption that has very little truth to it. Additionally, some people think - *'If I have many friends then only I am cool else not'*. Hope you are resonating with these thoughts. There are likely many more similar thoughts that generate unnecessary fear and anxiety. This is all due to our assumptions. It's a human tendency to assume when we don't know the facts, and this happens because we fail to ask questions—questions that could lead us to the truth. Questions which can lead us to reality. And, reality is bitter. Our assumptions seem sweet initially that we fall for them but unfortunately, they are worthless. They stop us from moving forward and let us stuck wherever we are. Just break this assumptions pattern and challenge these thoughts by considering the evidence. Is it really true that no one loves me or is it just my imagination? Are people really rejecting me when I speak or is there any other reason? Without evidence, even the law cannot pass judgment, so why are you being so judgmental about yourself based solely on assumptions? Get the facts. Attend gatherings. Meet people and check yourself. Are they really rejecting you or not? Start talking to someone close to you about yourself and check whether they really think you are weird or not. Check. Check and Check. Just don't assume. Be more aware about the real situation.

PURPOSEFUL LONELINESS

"

Loneliness is not a lack of company. Loneliness is a lack of PURPOSE.

"

GUILLERMO MALDONADO

Purpose word itself find its roots in Old French *purposer* which means to put (*poser*) forward (*pur*). Simply, it means to propose. A proposal to *self*. Entire life we tend to propose others, be it our lover, official partner, spouse or friend, to fulfil our various purposes but have we ever thought of proposing to ourselves? Never. It sounds weird but this proposal actually gives shape to our purposeful loneliness and helps us convert it into loveliness. It's amazing how one small letter can change the meaning of an entire word.

Whatever we do, there is an intent attached. If we go to school, we have an intent of getting educated. If we are getting married, there is an intention of companionship and taking our generation ahead. If we are on a vacation, we are there to derive leisure. We cannot move unless and until we have intent and purpose. So, if we feel isolated, estranged and forsaken, it is directly related to our *lack of purpose*. Consider the example of a sailboat that is directionless and does not know its destination. Will it ever reach the shore safely? You know the answer, but why won't it reach safely? Along its path, there are perils like unpredictable winds and currents. Enormous weather changes, storms, and hazardous waters can drift the boat aimlessly, preventing it from reaching the shore safely. The same logic applies to us. We feel lonely because we are directionless. We don't know where we are heading. Our intent is not strong or its entirely missing. This poses threat to our happiness and peace. This makes us so delicate and vulnerable that any tough situation can break us easily. Anyone can come along and hurt us. We need to be strong and that strength lies in having a *purpose*. As I write this, I am also alone—no one else is around. My room has only me as a living being. I can hear the sound of the fan clearly and see the curtains wavering. Yet, I am not fearful or anxious. In fact, I feel fulfilled inside. Do you know why? Because I have a purpose in my life: the purpose of writing and reaching out to millions of friends like you. My intent is to help those with beautiful souls and pure hearts and to guide them in finding the right direction in their lives.

What do you want to achieve when you have time for yourself or when you are alone? Identify an objective that can engage you consistently—something bigger in your life. This could be accumulating a specific amount of wealth (like 1 crore, 10 crore, or more) or perhaps learning a skill that could help you win an Olympic medal. If these goals feel too ambitious, you can set other goals that resonate with your ethics and morals. The idea is to find direction, and that direction will keep us engaged in working toward the achievement of our goals. That goal becomes the purpose of life. When we focus and work diligently on our goals, do you think there will be any space left for fear and anxiety? No, there won't be. In those moments, your purpose will be with you, and that purpose will never let you feel alone. You can work on your self-discovery, personal growth, creative expression, or simply peace and relaxation. You can utilise your aloneness for journaling, meditation, or pursuing a hobby. What this will do, it will add a meaning to your solitude and help you in transforming your loneliness into purposeful loneliness.

INTERNAL DESIRE TOWARD LONELINESS

Love is very important in life. If you don't love something, you end up losing it. In the same way, if you don't love your alone time, it won't benefit you. You will eventually end up losing these precious moments. Loving your loneliness means cultivating an internal desire for this feeling and making it productive for yourself. Let me ask you this: Will love flourish in an environment where fear prevails? Can trust thrive in an atmosphere dominated by suspicion? No. Not at all. So, how can one think of finding purpose in fearful conditions? It's like trying to bring the like poles of two magnets together—it will never happen. One has to leave the hem of one to embrace the other. You can either live in fear or in love, but not both. In my view, love is the better choice.

We need to develop an open mind-set toward aloneness and always be curious about taking time for ourselves. This is the opposite of what we were doing before. We used to view loneliness as a punishment or a sign of failure. The thought of being alone made us anxious, but now we must change our attitude toward it. We need to learn to love our alone time. Only then will we be able to embrace it and find our true purpose. Having said this, I know it's not easy. Writing words in a book is simple, but actually putting them into practice is a much harder task. It requires going through a wide range of emotions. You might be experiencing some of those feelings right now, and I completely understand—I've been through the same myself. I was once the same—fearful, withdrawn from the world, and anxious most of the time. I even felt envious of others. In 2017, I went through a difficult phase. For two months, I had no job. I had been working in Uttar Pradesh, but due to urgent family matters, I had to return to my hometown in Haryana. This meant leaving my job without another offer in hand. I had been earning a good income, but suddenly, it became zero. Around the same time, my wife left me, taking our daughter with her. I was completely alone. Although my elderly parents were with me, you can imagine how it felt—no job, no wife, no child. It was a tough time, but I didn't lose hope. I've always had a positive attitude toward life, and this mind-set really helped me during such a difficult time. I kept trying and set a clear goal for myself: to call at least 20 job consultants every day. I followed this plan religiously. My hard work paid off, and I landed a job at a fantastic organization with an even higher salary than before. On top of that, during those two months, I built a strong network of people, which continued to benefit me in the years that followed. All of this happened because of my internal desire not to let the difficult situation overpower me. I did feel anxious at times, but my passion and curiosity were stronger. I could have taken things personally and told myself, "Nobody loves me, no one cares about me," but those words are pessimistic. They only bring feelings of anger and frustration. Instead, I said to myself, "So what if nobody loves me? I love myself." And it was this self-love that helped me get my life back on track

A motivation to change and a commitment to yourself are the two key attributes that can help develop this internal desire. Instead of seeing the situation as a punishment, view it as an opportunity. Love the process rather than feeling like it's forced upon you. Always support it with plenty of hope and enthusiasm. Actively engage in practices and activities that align with your goals for solitude. Consider activities such as cooking, reading, walking, gardening, learning new skills, pursuing hobbies, painting, playing an instrument, meditating, journaling, creating videos, and more. The list is endless, as are the opportunities. The great news is that these opportunities are presented to us by our very own loneliness. So, set your intentions, hug your alone time, and make wonderful use of it.

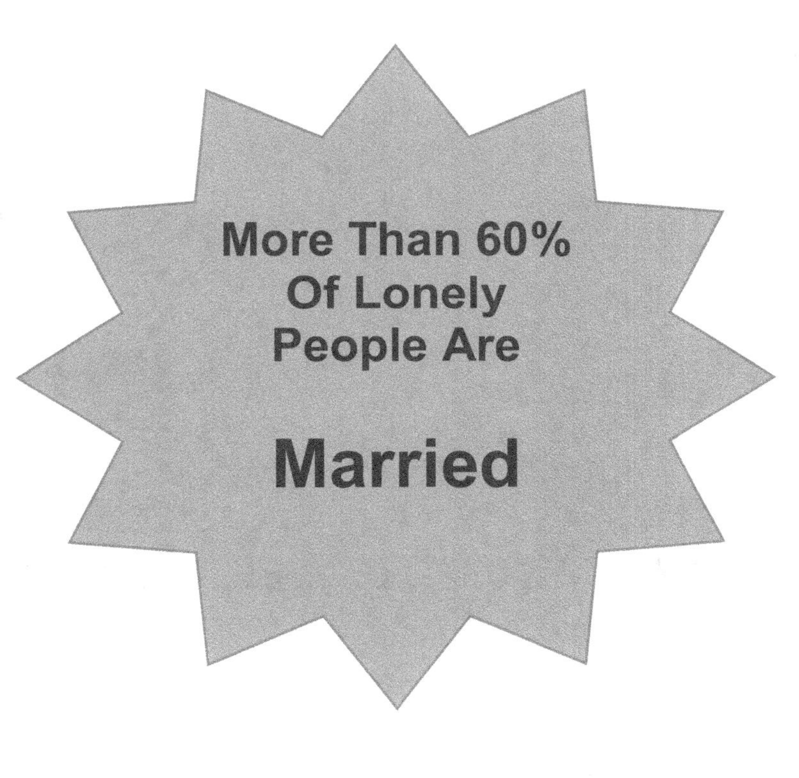

More Than 60%
Of Lonely
People Are

Married

4.
REFRAMING THE DEFINITION

D O YOU KNOW the relationship between the words "united" and "untied"? Yes, they are opposites, but there's something interesting about them: they are both made up of the same letters. Similarly, "stressed" and "desserts" form a wonderful antigram pair as well. You may be wondering what has suddenly come over me and why I'm discussing antigrams. The fascinating aspect of these words is their *essence*. They originate from the same letters, yet when rearranged, they convey opposite meanings. This is precisely what we need to do as we establish a strong foundation for transitioning from seclusion to solitude.

Both seclusion and solitude convey similar meanings, and their underlying principle is the same: being alone. However, they are far apart in their connotations, much like the North and South Poles. There is a stark difference. But, how can we distinguish between them? It's just like trying to differentiate chimpanzees and bonobos. They both look quite similar in appearance, but what separates them is their demeanor. Chimpanzees are much more aggressive in nature and have been known to engage in violent behaviour whereas Bonobos are known for being peaceful and resolving conflict through social bonding and play. This difference in character plays a crucial role in distinguishing between loneliness and aloneness.

Life is all about evolution, and change is inevitable. History provides a compelling testament to this, showing how humans have evolved from the cognitive age to the agricultural age, the industrial age, and now the digital age. We are still evolving and moving toward an artificial age. Therefore, we need to change how we perceive our alone time and reframe its definition. Otherwise, change will reshape it on its own, leaving us as mere spectators. Life is not about being a spectator, watching from the side-lines; it's about fully living and experiencing it. Therefore, whatever life offers, accept it with grace and relish it completely. However, the question still remains: how can we reframe our alone time?

If you've noticed, what do we contemplate when we are alone? In other words, when we are idle, what activity are we truly engaged in? Answer is *Nothing but Overthinking*. We become judgmental, analyse everything, and become our own toughest critics. We could easily fit in as members of the panel that selects the best actor or actress in a critic's role, don't you think? We don't spare anyone—be it our parents, siblings, friends, colleagues, neighbours, and, last but not least, we don't spare ourselves either. But what is the root cause of our overthinking? It's thinking itself. In his insightful book, *Don't Believe Everything You Think*, author Joseph Nguyen states "Thoughts create. Thinking destroys". He emphasizes that thinking is both the beginning and the end of all your suffering. Thus, the root cause of our loneliness lies in our thinking. He further explains that thoughts are divine because they connect us to our divine power, as we receive them from the universe. However, when we start thinking about those thoughts, we become critical, doubtful & judgemental. As a result, we break our connection with our divinity through our thinking and that is when our suffering begins. Hence, we need to reduce the span of time we spend thinking each day and focus more on being in *flow*. We should approach every task with a *rhythm* that leaves very little time for overthinking. When we establish a process and concentrate on executing it, we create a routine. By adhering to a particular regimen for a certain period, it becomes ingrained in our behaviour and starts to feel automatic.

30/90 RULE

Once, I attended a workshop on good habits, where I learned about the golden rule for creating a habit and making it autonomous. This rule says that anything you do *religiously* for 30 days continuous, it becomes a habit and then, if you continue that practice for 90 days, then it becomes a lifestyle. Easy, right? Read again. You must follow this activity like a religion and ensure that, just as you thank the Almighty every day without needing a reminder, you perform this activity consistently without any breaks in between. Continuity is key, and maintaining this continuity will help you achieve *rhythm or flow*. It could be anything, such as a 15-minute workout, brushing your teeth twice daily, writing one page, reading ten pages, learning a new skill, or playing a sport for one hour. Have you noticed something here? All of these are specific statements with a clear number attached to each activity—15, 2, 1, 10, and 1. This specificity adds meaning to your efforts, demonstrating that you are serious and committed to your goals. This approach will help you move away from vagueness and significantly boost your productivity. Make sure you engage in any of these activities, or even ones of your own choosing, for *30-continuous* days. It doesn't matter what excuses come to mind,

Today is Sunday, let me skip today, or

I'm not feeling 100%, I'll do it tomorrow, or

I don't have enough time to do it properly today.

you have to do it for 30 days continuously. You will notice a change in yourself well before the 30th day arrives. But what comes next? Should we stop? Is that it? Have we done enough? No, absolutely not. Get up and continue the same activity for another 60 days. Human nature tends to revert to lethargy and seek comfort if left unattended. That initial 30 days of hard work will be in vain if you don't continue for the next 60 days. This is why most people leave gyms and clubs within the first month of enrolment—they expect instant results and often don't stick with it. But those who persevere uncover the hidden magic. The next 60 days will transform your routine into autopilot mode, so ingrained in your subconscious that even on days when you don't feel like exercising, your subconscious will take over and help you carry out the activity. After 90 days, if you want to take a break for one day every ten days or so, you can afford to do so because your internal system is established, and that process is now set.

I follow the same regime. Till last year, I was not exercising but now I have instilled 15-min workout daily in my morning schedule and even if it is Sunday or holiday, I will work out. It has become automatic now. When I work, I take multiple short breaks instead of longer ones, as longer breaks can disrupt my flow and lead to overthinking. By staying in the *groove*, I achieve better results.

Till now we have been contemplating a lot about how we could modify ourselves internally but our internal system alone cannot function efficiently if our external ecosystem is in poor shape. We need to take care of everything that is in our vision which can create a sense of fear and anxiety in us. For instance, if we see our home or workplace unorganised, if everything is haphazardly placed (or misplaced), if nothing is in order, will we be able to settle down properly and invite beautiful ideas? No chance. Stuff like Keys, pens, headphones, earbuds, remote controls, coins, receipts, bills, hair ties, clips, batteries, post-it notes, glasses, sunglasses, charging cables, USB drives, old magazines, newspapers, jewellery, envelopes, empty shopping bags, toys, mobile chargers, scissors, nail-cutters, books, bottles, containers, wrappers and on and on and on. Huff! Even while writing this I am feeling overwhelmed and I am certain you are feeling the same too. With so many trivial things taking up your precious life space, how can you breathe harmoniously? What's more concerning is that this disorganized environment adds to your fear of loneliness, as it makes you feel stuck in a big box with hardly any space around you. This is the major reason why most people feel suffocated inside. The solution lies both in front of them and around them. Clear you mess around. Put everything in its designated place. Make everything organised and in order. Your table, all drawers, your kitchen, washroom, closet, bedside table, countertops, shelves, living room, garage, car, desk, wardrobe, coffee table, bathroom cabinet, pantry, laundry room, shoe rack, attic, and storage boxes. Ensure everything is in proper shape. I know you are feeling swamped but this is a one-time activity. Trust me, once it's done you will fall in love with your place. Just ensure, you follow the strict discipline of keeping everything at its designated place only. 30/90 rule will surely help you in this.

Once done, you will automatically feel freed and breezy. There will be an openness in your environment which will further open up your mind for beautiful thoughts. Openness reminds me of people who feel lonely and secluded. I have seen people who experience loneliness, they try to keep their doors, windows and curtains closed. They feel fearful that if doors are open, somebody will come and harm them. If they are packed, then only they are safe and secure. Even when they sleep, they contract their body and don't sleep with calmness. Even they hold their bedsheets very closely and tightly. How I could say all this with so much certainty is because I have seen *myself* behaving in the similar manner. As a child, I felt afraid and lonely so I mostly kept my room door closed. My mother often asked me to open the door but I didn't, out of fear. This continued for a few years until I realized that this is all a game created by our mind, and it plays with us. Our loneliness is often influenced by our thoughts and perceptions, and here our mind can amplify these feelings based on our life experiences. Then I started working on myself and first thing which I did was *open the door*. Yes, I became more receptive to new ideas and thoughts keep pouring on its own once I stepped out of my box-like life. I became more action-oriented and left very little scope for overthinking. Not only did I open the door to my room, but I also did the same for my mind. I also invite you to do the same right now. Go open the door or window and let the freshness breeze in. Go out and feel the air. Embrace the fragrance of nature. Listen to the magical sounds of god's creation. If it's night, gaze at the stars and sense every bit of wonderful darkness. You will automatically start feeling light, confident and energetic.

Create a dedicated place in your *newly organized* home for your alone time. Whether it's a corner, a small room, or a backyard, it should be yours and yours alone. Aim to spend at least a scheduled time each day in this newly found habitat—a physical space where you can retreat and feel comfortable being alone. To make it more vibrant, you can surround your place with objects that brings positivity and joy to you such as books, plants, artwork, motivational quotes and calendars. You can also light incense sticks as a ritual to create a soothing atmosphere, to ward off worries and invite positive, aesthetic thoughts.

All of this is very much possible, but one must back themselves. It will not happen overnight, and negative thinking will not disappear immediately. Change occurs slowly and gradually over time, requiring continuous and sustained efforts in the right direction. *Visualisation* plays an imperative role here in creating this positive frame of mind. We have to envision ourselves happy in our imagination, only then will we work toward that happiness. You would agree that every significant achievement was once just a thought, a product of our imagination. And, these thoughts are divine (as we discussed earlier). But, when we keep ruminating on these thoughts for longer periods to time, they become a worry. Hence, we need to remain calm and free from anxieties. We should encourage our minds to generate more thoughts, and once we receive them, rather than being critical, we should engage with them positively. This visualisation is another aspect of reframing our definition of loneliness. Earlier, we used to think negatively about alone time. Even the mere thought of being alone would send shivers down our spine. But not anymore. Now that we understand it's all about mind-set, we can rearrange our thoughts in a more positive way. By doing so, we can develop a healthier pattern that makes us stronger and more cheerful than ever before.

Congratulations! You are half way through. You must be feeling a lot lighter and insightful by now. Well-deserved pat on your back! By this point, you've done significant groundwork and laid a strong foundation. You've likely begun to accept loneliness and see it as a companion rather than an adversary. Now, it's time to move beyond mere acceptance and into incorporation. In the next section, we'll explore how to actively integrate solitude into your daily life. This is where loneliness transforms from something to endure into a powerful tool for personal growth.

All set? Superb. Let's move ahead!

PART III.
Incorporation

5.
SELF - REFLECTION

"

Only in still water do we see the depth of our reflection.

"

WHY DO WE behave in a particular situation, the way we behave? Why do we think the way we do most of the time?

And, why do we say the way we say? These *whys* are so critical to our self-discovery, yet we often overlook them altogether. Uncertainty is another name for life. Whenever we attempt to settle down, life throws some challenge our way, leaving us completely perplexed. Throughout our lives, we strive for certainty about various things, people, and situations, yet we often forget to seek certainty within ourselves. We often feel anxious when things are unclear in our lives, such as our school grades, job roles, salary increases, or tax deductions. However, what's even more profound and critical is that we frequently overlook the need to inquire about ourselves.

One day, I was driving with my 12-year-old daughter when it started to rain. The windscreen became blurry, but every time I turned on the wipers, it cleared up. My daughter, watching this, was fascinated and said, "This clarity looks so good". Any older individual can relate to this when they clear the lenses of their spectacles. This highlights a universal truth: regardless of age, gender, caste, or race, we all seek clarity in our lives. This clarity is what enables us to move forward. But how can we attain clarity in our lives when our minds are clouded and occupied by worries, fears, doubts, criticisms, resentments, and uncertainties? Its answer lies in *simplicity*.

Charlie Chaplin once said "Simplicity is not a simple thing", and how incredibly accurate he was. It's ironic that we often pursue happiness by accumulating more, while true prosperity actually comes from letting go of what we don't need in our lives. Simplicity lies in accepting circumstances, people, emotions, challenges, experiences, outcomes, events, realities, relationships, differences, flaws, and most importantly, life *as it is*. But it's our mind which plays the spoilsport and tries to make things complex for us. It does not let us relax and always push us toward analysing everything around. It makes us so much judgemental that we don't even spare ourselves. We are god's unique creation and yet we don't understand that. We get totally lost in the opinions and judgements of people around us who have no clue of what's going inside us but still we believe them. Any guesses why? Because we are not *still* inside. In other words, our inner wisdom is so much muddled and we are not able to see our own shadow in that turbulence of life. This is the reason why self-reflection is so imperative. This reflection is nothing but looking ourselves with calmness and thoughtfulness. This self-consideration can provide us the much-needed insight of ourselves which could lead us to the path of enlightenment. But how many of us actually do this self-consideration? Very few.

To clarify my point, allow me to share an analogy. Imagine yourself to be a sculptor who has a big block of unshaped marble. You have a task of turning that block into a fine piece of artwork. But throughout your work time you are surrounded by people with their unlimited opinions. Will you be able to complete that task aesthetically? No. With all noise and distractions your focus is scattered and with this you can never make any progress. In simple words, your mind is not clear and hence you cannot complete that task on time. Now imagine you have a workplace where you are all alone and there is nobody to bother you. In this alone time, you finally have much desired space and with this you attain peace of mind. With this stillness of mind, you are able to see the shape hidden in the piece of marble. With each stroke of chisel that artistic figure starts to emerge in front of your eyes. What has happened here? In this peaceful and reflective environment, you are able to listen to your inner artist properly, *free* from any noise. This block of marble is nothing but your inner self – your identity. With external pressures, it becomes very difficult to listen your inner music but when you step into solitude, you gain the time and space to carefully "sculpt" your identity. Everything boils down to one thing – simplifying the life. And, this simpler life further helps in attaining much needed space and time with oneself that is essential in attaining solitude.

HOW TO ATTAIN SIMPLICITY?

By incorporating oneness.

"

One multiplied by One is equal to One.

"

Our life is loaded with multiple types of mathematical equations which includes additions, multiplications, percentages, sequences, compounding and so on. We believe in adding more and more and then try to multiply and multiply. But the true essence of life and happiness lies in *oneness* (simplicity) and not making it big and complex. How often we see affluent people even after acquiring tons of wealth still feels unfulfilled and finally find solace in living simple life and doing charity. Many famous celebrities turn to spirituality and simplicity after reaching the peak of their fame and success. Prominent individuals such as Richard Gere embracing Buddhism, Angelina Jolie working toward humanitarian work and environmental causes, and Steve jobs wearing simple clothes everyday shows how being simple is the only way to connect to inner wisdom and universe. Oneness reduces the sense of separation between us and others. It further helps in uniting us with ourselves by letting go of unnecessary complications and worries, and finally embracing infinite abundance (Divinity).

Simplicity encourages self-reflection. When both internal and external distractions are removed that clutter our mind and life, we would be able to see within ourselves. We could feel ourselves. Whatever thoughts we receive from the universe, we would be able to embrace them without any criticism and judgement. Author Renuka Gavrani in her profound meaning book *The Art of Being Alone*, writes 'When you are alone, you are dealing with just one mind, one set of choices, behaviours and thinking patterns. Hence, it becomes easier to study yourself and get to know what you like and what you don't like, how you think and how you react.' What beautiful lines these are! They simply and clearly convey that aloneness is the only path to self-discovery. Here, too, the power of *one* is highlighted. This power of one is nothing but God. When we set aside all forms of complexity and embrace oneness in its simplest form, we will discover peace, love, and joy. In other words, we will find both ourselves and God. This embodies the true meaning of (1 x 1 =1) i.e. Simplicity x Self = God.

What have we done here? We have simply *stated the problem.* We have expressed life's meaning in its purest form. We have maintained the pristinity and sacredness of life. This comprehension of life takes us to the fact that we cannot control things. There is a divine power above us who has the ultimate authority but we innocent beings think we are in control of everything. We resist change whereas it is inevitable. We simply need to accept life as it is and move with its flow, because when we are in flow, we are in our most natural state. What is this natural state or state of non-thinking? It's nothing but *the present moment.* Whenever we are thinking, we are never truly in the present. We are either lost in the past or anxious about the future. What's interesting is that neither the past nor the future actually exists—they're both uncontrollable. Yet, we find ourselves absorbed in these states for much of our lives. On the contrary, when we stop thinking, we become mindful. We focus on what's happening around us in the present moment. We can fully sense the finer details of the world—flavours, fragrances, sounds, textures, and sights. Just retrospect, whenever you feel alone, anxious or fearful, do you sense any of these details? No. But, why? They all exist with you. It's because you are not in your natural state of being. You are completely overwhelmed by negative emotions, which entirely encapsulate you. This feeling is what we call loneliness. Now, if you let go of all of your negative emotions by stop thinking, then you'll naturally return to your inherent state of well-being. In that current moment, you are fully aware of what's happening and what's real, rather than getting lost in a world of illusion. This state is known as aloneness or solitude.

TRIGGERS AND PATTERNS

Every human state of being is precipitated by a trigger and shaped by patterns. Trigger is an event that occurs before a feeling and influence it whereas pattern is a repeated response to that event or trigger. One very common example nowadays that provokes loneliness among almost everyone is, scrolling through social media and watching videos and pictures of others enjoying. This is not entirely wrong to watch others enjoy and get inspiration from them but it is taken adversely. Watching others engage in leisurely activities of partying, traveling, laughing et cetera often aggravates the feeling that we are left out. This over a period of time lead to the feelings of inadequacy. This gives birth to the feelings that others have more fulfilling lives and we don't belong to that group. We tend to ignore these feelings initially but deep down it hurt us. We fake that we don't care about these but actually even after turning the social media off we use to think about it only. Here social media is the trigger and over the period of time shapes the pattern. So, whenever we pick up the phone later on, it triggers the mode of loneliness. Other triggers could be any change in climatic conditions such as many individuals fear from clouds as it becomes dark and sunshine goes away, so they tend to move inside alone rather than enjoying the cool breeze. Many others fear bigger crowds so whenever they witness large gatherings it evokes the feeling of anxiousness and fear in them. Whatever it is, there is a trigger or a sign that tells us that we are going into that hindrance mode and we need to identify it.

Acknowledge the sign which is causing you this feeling. First of all, you need to be aware of the fact that this particular activity is the root cause. Next time, whenever you will feel alone, just be mentally prepared to check on what happened *right before* this feeling. Was it a sad song that triggered the event, or going to a particular place that made you remember someone? Or an old photograph? Or what? You need to go into very fine details and be as concrete as possible. In other words, you need to *tangibilise* your problem. If the problem is identified, then only you could be prescribed a remedy. You could also pen down the series of events and check yourself the pattern around it. See, this sounds a little weird but trust me this is much better than the weirdness you are already suffering (seclusion). What this activity brings, it will bring you back to the current moment - to the present. It will help you shake-hand with the reality and this gesture will infuse a lot of confidence inside you.

Now that, you have identified the problem and stated it right in front of you, you will start to feel much better and lighter. In percentage terms if I talk about, 80% you will be relieved. But, what about the 20%? This remaining 20% will be released by taking action on it. One ritual which I personally follow in my life is, whatever fear I have to remove from my life, I immediately go and encounter it. Simply stating, whatever I think will make me fearful, I do that only and that too right away. My biggest fear was speaking on a stage so one day I decided to get over this fear and participated in an event. That dissipated my fear forever and this gave me lot of confidence. Honesty speaking, it was not easy and it took my years to gather that courage but I encourage you not to wait for years like me and participate in any of the event whether personal, professional or social to get over your similar fear of speaking in crowd. Other fear of mine was starting a conversation with anyone. For years, I was not able to talk to a person I liked just because of lack of courage and positive attitude. What I do now is quickly start with a greeting and then follow up with a compliment to that person. Obviously a genuine one! What this has done is it has helped me make many new friends and acquaintances and with them around I don't feel alone anymore. If anyone criticizes me, I ask them straightway and resolve the issue. If I have done anything wrong, I apologise on the spot. I don't wait, crib and distort my mental peace. If I have any health issue, I immediately go and consult a physician and get it sorted. If I have to invest in any plan, I research on it, analyse my risk appetite accordingly and if it allows, I invest in it right away. This keeps me financially safe and happy. So, whatever the disease (fear), there is a medicine (action) accordingly. But, the task is to go and take that medicine and much before that disease needs to be diagnosed. That's it. It's that simple. I cordially invite you to grace the occasion (Your life) and take these remedial steps promptly to live a smooth, fearless, and fulfilling life of solitude.

To summarise, whenever we feel lonely we need to accept the fact, welcome the feeling and embrace it with both hands. This feeling is transmitted to us by the divinity and to help us become a better version of ourselves rather than getting into the state of fear and trepidness. Whenever we face any kind of challenge we need to just sit down, relax and state the problem. This state of calmness will bring the much desired *transparency* which will further clear all the doubts and bring us closer to the solution.

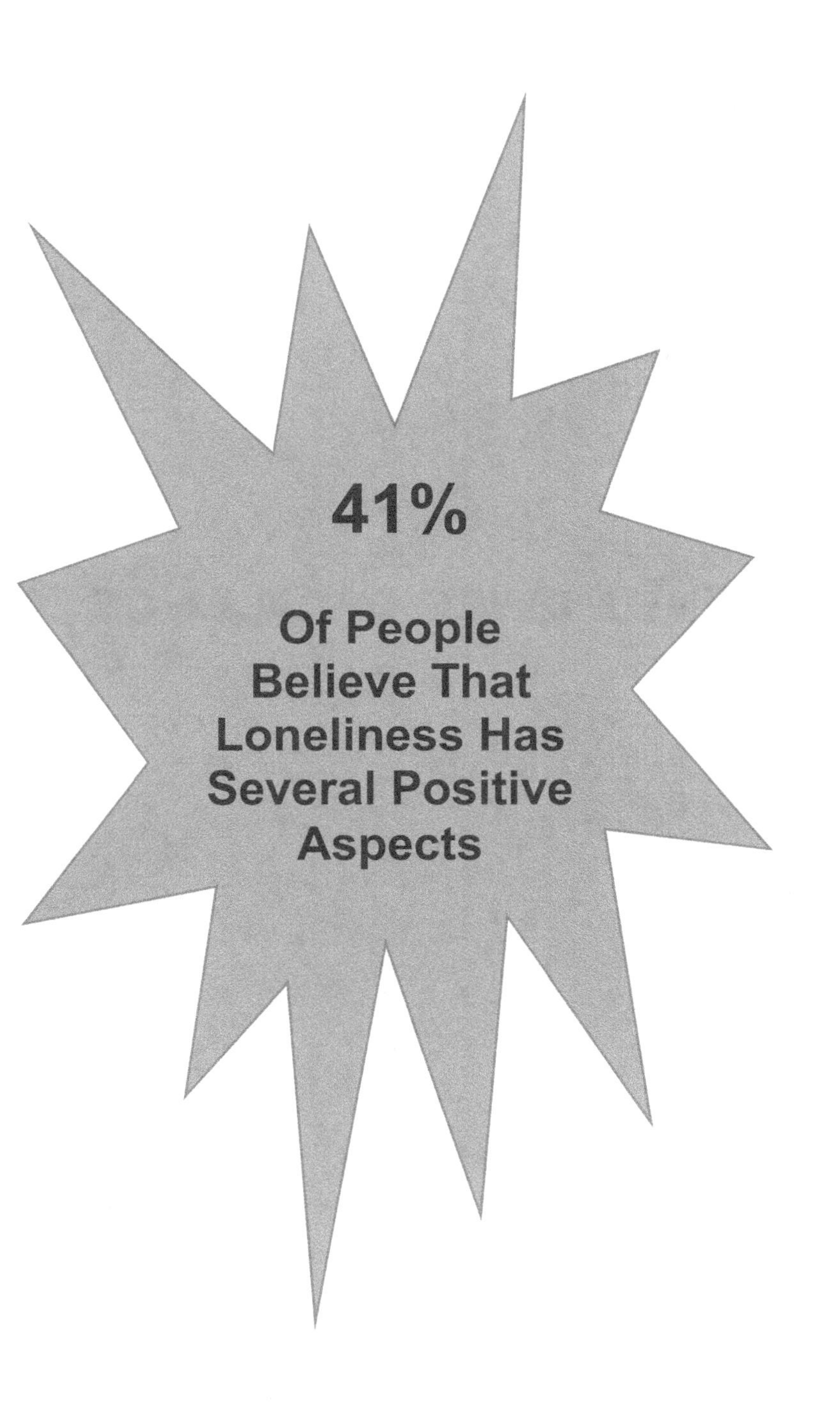

41%

Of People
Believe That
Loneliness Has
Several Positive
Aspects

6.
THE POWER OF SILENCE

> "
>
> *The unknown always passes for the marvellous.*
>
> "

DO YOU BELIEVE in *nothing*? Do you feel afraid to step into the *unknown*? Do you like the concept of *Zeros*?

The reason I'm asking these questions at the start of this chapter is that we are about to enter an unfamiliar zone – the Zone of the Unknown. What makes us fearful of the unchartered territory - Is it the uncertainty or the unfamiliarity of something we don't know? Or is it related to our biological evolution? Or perhaps it is shaped by our past encounters with the unknown? Well, the reasons could be many but the real reason why we don't step into the undiscovered passage is, excitement. Or should I say, *too much of excitement.* This 'too much' manifests as anxiety because we tend to overthink the issue. Additionally, as we learned in the previous chapter, overthinking is often the root cause of our suffering. We keep howling outside rather than gathering the courage to check what's inside. We bombard our minds with irrelevant assumptions that serve no real purpose and only deepen our misery. This is why many people fear marriage. Even though they believe they understand it by observing married couples around them, the thought of actually experiencing it themselves sends shivers down their spine. Similar feelings of uncertainty arise when people consider changing jobs or moving to a foreign country, even when these changes could greatly benefit them. Yet, they still prefer to remain where they are. But why? Why do we behave this way when we know deep down that it could benefit us? The answer is *comfort*. We're not ready to let go of our comfort, even when we know it could bring significant rewards. This rationale is further reinforced by the fear of the unknown. Although we understand that taking a step into the unknown can offer us greater rewards, there's also a significant chance it could go other way. If we decide to leave our current tedious job for a better opportunity, there's a possibility that this new venture could turn out to be even more challenging. We can offer ourselves countless explanations for why we shouldn't move toward unexplored territories, but we cannot deny that our true potential lies in this 'Zone of the Unknown', waiting to be discovered.

Why, at times, do we feel that we are not moving at all? Why our saturation limits are reached too quickly? It's because we set our limits *too low*. We keep ourselves smaller targets fearing of the bigger ones. After reaching our goals easily, we may feel happy for a brief moment, but that sense of fulfilment is never truly attained. True fulfilment surfaces only when we venture into the pool of the unknown. We believe in a divine power or infinite intelligence that governs our every action. But have we ever seen it? No. Yet we still trust it. This divine power, this sense of divinity, is nothing but the *unknown*. Everything begins with this one power and eventually returns to it. Although this power remains unknown to us, we continue to believe in it, holding onto the hope that God is with us. This belief in ourselves can be further strengthened and reinforced through 'The Power of Silence'.

WHAT IS THE POWER OF SILENCE?

Let us understand this with a saga of an emperor and the silent sage. Once upon a time, there was a wise emperor. He was widely known for his wisdom and valour. But despite such gallantry he didn't felt fulfilled. He consulted his ministers and one of them suggested him to pay a visit to a legendary sage who lived far away in the mountains of seclusion. Without wasting any time, the king started his journey to visit the sage to gain insight. Finally, after a long and arduous journey, the king reached at the sage's humble hut. After the greetings, the king almost in desperation asked, "Wisdom figure, what is the secret to true leadership and inner peace?". The sage remained silent. After few moments, he took the emperor to a nearby small, tranquil stream flowing near his hut. They sat there for many hours without saying a single word. This frustrated the king and out of high level of curiosity, he said to the sage, "Why are we sitting here in silence and why have you not answered my question?". The sage still remained silent. Considering this as a contempt of his, the emperor decided to leave out of anger. The sage then smiled gently and said, "The answer to your question lies in the quietness of your heart and not in the sound of the words". The king sat down again and started to feel the calmness around. He observed the gentle flow of the stream. He felt the peaceful surroundings. This provide him profound sense of calm and clarity. He realized that silence is the only way that could reveal him the answers to his questions and the path to fulfilment can only be enlightened with the clarity and wisdom that comes from within.

Ironically, we associate power with noise and sounds of glory, war, triumph, and grand speeches whereas deep strength lies in quietude and contemplation. We run after the world for success and fulfilment but the real success lies within us. We look for connections with outside world, failing which drags us to the sea of sad emotions (loneliness) but we often overlook the importance of connecting with self which can actually elevate us to the heights of solitude and self-discovery. But, why we don't connect with ourselves more often than not when this silence is so impactful? The answer to this timeless question lies in realisation and freedom. We don't realise that answers to our queries can be found within. We doubt this *unknown* area of our soul, leading us to seek resolutions outside ourselves. Another reason we struggle to connect with ourselves is that we often don't feel free. We bind ourselves to so many material possessions and emotions that we constantly feel weighed down. In simpler terms, we don't feel free because we *hold on to too much.*

Newton's first law of motion says "*An object in motion stays in motion, and an object at rest stays at rest, unless acted upon by an external force.*" This holds true for our existence as a being also, that if we are in a state of flow or rhythm then we continue to stay in that motion only unless we put force of doubts, fears, or negative thoughts to disrupt this flow and create resistance. These external forces influence our progress and well-being. Similarly, when we are in loneliness state, if we don't apply any force of positivity, hopefulness and self-compassion, then we sink deeper and deeper into the swamp of isolation and despair. The Power of Unknown or Power of Silence is something that can help us maintain a flow of positivity and during times of adversity, embracing silence or the unknown can guide us through challenges and bring us back on the path of self-discovery.

"

*I think 99 times and find nothing. I stop thinking,
swim in silence, and the truth comes to me.*

"

Albert Einstein

INCORPORATING MINDFULNESS

What is the essence of mindfulness? It's to be in the present moment *completely.* Fully present. Conscious. But, it is the most challenging part of our lives to be *present* in the present. Whatever we do from dawn to dusk is simply - reflect, contemplate, and ponder - endlessly thinking. When we are freshening up, we are reflecting. When we are brushing our teeth, we are contemplating. When we are eating, we are musing. When we are driving, we are considering. If we are in a meeting, we start deliberating. When attending a class, we start pondering. Leave everything else—even during moments of intimacy, we are still speculating. And what do we derive out of this endless thinking? Nothing. One day I reached office and one of my colleague asked, "what happened to your hair?". I said nothing. But when I saw mirror I realised that I forgot to comb. And, this was not the first time. It happened lot many times before because I was totally lost ruminating about past and future. Since morning till night my day was spent in over analysing – about personal life, career, health, relationships, targets, promotions, finances, debt, investments, hobbies, travel and so on. I am sure I am not alone in this world dwelling on thoughts like these. Almost everyone is doing the same. To be honest, it's not our fault either. We have been programmed this way since childhood. Listen to others, obey elders, help fellow people, work hard for grades, compete and stay ahead of others, run fast else you will be left behind. This is what embedded in us day in and day out. But no one taught us to follow our heart, to listen to our inner music. Nobody said that its ok if you are behind, at least you are happy. Nobody told us that life has unlimited options. Therefore, don't be concerned if you find yourself doing the same. There is a way out. Adopt mindfulness. And, silence provides more than a helpful hand in accepting it.

When we are alone, it is the best opportunity God has presented to us. It's just a matter of realising this. When surrounded by people, noise and distractions, we tend to forget ourselves. We cannot listen to our inner wisdom. We are influenced by the opinions of others. Loneliness is a golden opportunity to welcome silence and incorporate mindfulness. This state of inner stillness helps in deep soul shift which further brings profound wisdom and tranquillity. The calmness of mind helps in observing our thoughts without judgment and with greater clarity. It is a time to reprogram ourselves and transform into a new version of ourselves. Silence creates the much-needed *space* inside us, essential for moving forward. To create anything, space is essential. If we can attain this space through silence, our progress is assured. How this space is created is when we stop overthinking and are in our natural state of existence, allowing us to find our *groove*. We are neither in past nor in future. We are in current moment. No judgements, no opinions, no distractions. We are completely *us* and this is when a beautiful space is created inside us which allows divine thoughts to surface. In this moment, we become aware of the sound of our breath, the beating of our heart, or the small sensations in our body.

HOW CAN THIS MINDFULNESS BE ACHIEVED PRACTICALLY?

Let's do a small activity first. Take two 1-Litre water bottles with *narrow* openings. Fill one with water and let the other empty. Now, pour the water from the filled bottle into the empty one. Done? What did you notice? You were silent throughout the process of pouring and were totally concentrating on the flow. You ensured that not a single drop of water was spilled. This is mindfulness. At that moment, you had no thoughts—neither negative nor positive— you were simply present and whole. This is the magic and beauty of silence and mindfulness. Now that we know what mindfulness looks like, let's explore how we can incorporate its magic and spread it across every aspect of our lives. How can we achieve this? Simply by *blending* it into every little activity of our daily routine.

- START WITH DAILY PRACTICE – Bruce Lee once said, "Practice makes perfect," but we are not pursuing perfection. We are aiming for mindfulness, and practice certainly helps with that too. Start your day with mindful activity such as focusing on your breath as soon as you wake up. Take a pause of 2 minutes and feel your breath completely by closing your eyes. Then be mindful while brushing your teeth and taking bath. Ensure you don't ruminate while doing these hygiene activities.

- MINDFUL COMMUNICATION – Take a pledge before entering your workplace that Today you will 'listen more and talk less'. Ensure you try to listen every word clearly by the person who meets you. This will bring empathy and patience in your interactions with others. Be totally aware and present in all meetings and replace your reactions with your responses. You can only be able to do this once you are mindful.

- CREATE MINDFUL MOMENTS – Take regular mindful *breaks* during the day. This is a way of getting feedback from your mind and body that you need to re-charge. You can use 20-20-20 rule, pomodoro technique or whatever suits you but it should be effective, regular and can help you refresh.

- SPREAD MINDFULNESS IN RELATIONSHIPS – When was the last time you listened to your child *attentively*? When was the last time you said 'Miss you' to your partner looking in their eyes? Usually, it's just a quick message sent during a lunch break, and that's it. Make it a routine. Listen to your child for at least 5 minutes, *putting aside* everything—work, the remote control, and your mobile phone. Children observe everything and will share their thoughts as they grow older. Don't let them hold onto any grudges. Hug them and truly listen. Give the same amount of time, if not more, to your partner, and you'll notice that the remaining 23.55 hours of your life will be more beautiful than ever.

- MINDFUL OBSERVATION – Pay close attention to everything around you. Observe the little details about (i) Nature - Notice how a squirrel hops and eats its food, and closely examine the patterns on a butterfly's wings. (ii) Food - Savour the colours, textures, and fragrances of your meal. Enjoy every bite. (iii) Movement – While driving, concentrate solely on the steering wheel, pedals, and rear-view mirrors, pushing aside any other thoughts. When walking, focus on each step and the sensations and movements of your body.

Silence is like a magician's wand, capable of transforming the scared into the sacred. It absorbs everything within itself, bringing balance to chaos and focus to distraction. It infuses serenity into the storm and insight into confusion. It offers peace amidst unrest and vision through the haze. If you are silent within, external turbulence will not disturb you. If you are happy inside, you'll remain content even in traffic; otherwise, frustration will creep in. When you focus, your inner calm can steady the wavering ship of your life. All that's needed is to be more aware and conscious. If you have a fever but don't acknowledge it, will you go to the doctor and take medicine? No. Similarly, only when you become aware of your inner wisdom and accept yourself as you are, can you truly move forward in bettering yourself. I hope I'm resonating with you.

With me?

This brings us to the end of this section. Take a moment to relax—breathe deeply, and remind yourself that you're doing amazing. By now, it goes without saying that you must be thoroughly enjoying this journey. I'm confident that you no longer feel the way you did when you first started this book, and I'm feeling great right along with you.

Before we move forward, I encourage you to flip back through the previous three sections and reflect on what you've learned so far. You've done incredible work, first by clearing the negativity from your life and accepting things as they are. Then, you laid a strong foundation by setting your intentions right, and you even redefined loneliness on your own terms—that was a remarkable achievement! In the third section, you engaged in deep self-reflection and integrated the power of the unknown into your personality.

All this wonderful progress brings us to the threshold of a complete transformation into a newer version of ourselves. This new self has been waiting for a long time—waiting for us to release it from its shell and set it free. Now is the time to fully step into your personal power and get every aspect of your life on track.

Are you ready to step into your newfound power?

PART IV.
Reincarnation

YES. IT'S A REBIRTH. A return of a soul who never wants to be same again. This is actually another version of yours who has learnt how to cope up with the intricacies of this world. This newer version knows how to deal with the people around. It knows how to transform challenges into opportunities. It also has the power to convert bitter experiences into fruitful ones with the laser sharp insight. This version is lot clearer, wiser and conscious, having attained wisdom from the betrayals, deceit and ill-treatment at the hands of so called 'near and the dear ones'. It's a shift from negative end (fear, anger, guilt) of the spectrum, called life, toward the positive end (kindness, confidence, peace). It sounds synonymous with a blockbuster movie where the main lead transforms from a humble, naive, and unassuming character into a witty, sharp, and astute personality.

Why 'reincarnation' is because it's a newer you. This version is all set to take your life to new heights and help you find the right path to success. A sense of inner calm and contentment, compared to the older self, will help you harness your true potential and help you evolve into a more purposeful and enlightened person than ever before. This evolution presents a fantastic opportunity to fulfil all your dreams, desires and aspirations into reality.

With a confident smile, let's march ahead.

7.
GOLDEN OPPORTUNITY

"

Do not try to do everything. Do one thing well.

"

Steve Jobs

WHEN WAS THE LAST TIME you spoke to your parents, siblings or old friends? I'm asking this because as we grow older, we often think we know it all and, in the process, we tend to drift away from those closest to us. Ones with whom we spent our childhood and golden moments of life, we often harbour some kind of resentments from them in the name of material things of life. It has happened to me and many others I know. It's a decision made in the heat of the moment, and we often regret it later. But even after realizing this, we don't visit or pick up our phone to reconnect because our so-called ego gets in the way. We keep waiting for the other person to *make the first move*, and this wait only creates a bigger emptiness inside us, giving our ego more room to grow. We come up with countless judgements and opinions to feed our ego, and before we know it, many years slip away. But not anymore. This is no longer the old version that keeps brooding over people and circumstances with blame. Now, it sees the situation clearly, understand it wisely, and make decisions in a positive direction that benefit everyone. It understands that peace of mind is far more important than winning. Now, saying sorry and apologizing isn't as hard, because there's a deep realization that meaningful relationships matter much more than unnecessary ego. This *unwanted distance* from relatives and friends is one of the biggest sources of stress and loneliness, and it can be resolved with just one step of courage. Once again, the power of *one* reminds us that we are always just one step away from peace and wisdom.

Multitasking is a good word but it cannot defeat the profound meaning of oneness. Use this newly attained wisdom and apply it wisely, improving one habit at a time. Start from one task or virtue to improve. If you successfully accomplish one task, it will automatically radiate to the other aspects of your life. For instance, to start with, if you have successfully maintained a regular exercise routine, you will automatically see an increase in your energy levels. This will result in better sleep and improved mood. It will further translate into your enhanced productivity and you will experience higher levels of happiness and peace. Another example could be proper financial planning. If you inculcate habit of saving and budgeting, then it could not only reduce your anxiety but also increase your overall sense of security. You will be on your path of achieving your life's goals (Travel, home, education, car et cetera) which will help you maintain harmonious relationships with others at home and workplace. It all starts from one.

One major feature of this path of *re-discovery* is confronting with the fear of failure. Whatever it is, whether we have attained enlightened perspective or deep faith in our abilities, we will always be humans. And, our minds will always try to drag us back to the world of doubts, uncertainties and fears. Since thousands of years our minds have been wired on the theme of just survival. It shows us ways to survive only and not to thrive. So we need to keep asking ourselves one question every time?

'Which failure are you?'

Are you the one who tries and fails or the one who always thinks and fails to try? This is a great query to self even if we are already on the path of freedom. And we should keep asking this whenever we feel down. Whenever the dark clouds of fears try to dampen our confidence we need to use this question as a shield to cope up and come up. I'm sure that since you've come this far, you are the first type and not the second. You trust your abilities and are always willing to try instead of just waiting on the side-lines. Loneliness is a golden opportunity because it holds a lot of undiscovered treasures beneath the surface. Life is like a goldmine, and those who trust, dig deep, have patience, and enjoy the process, will find success. Loneliness offers a great chance to unlock your hidden potential, but only for those who are willing to do so. Let's explore some real-life scenarios where we can turn our alone time into something golden.

PERSONAL GROWTH

Robert has shifted recently to a new city and feeling a sense of loneliness. It's his first time out for a job, and he is finding it difficult to cope with the pressures of life. The job also seems to be less interesting to him and all the adverse thoughts are passing thorough his mind. Rather than surrendering to these detrimental thoughts, he has started journaling. He has started writing down everything going on inside him, including his thoughts, memories, emotions, dreams, and desires. He does this every day without fail after work. What this has done is it has helped him peel layers of innate feelings and helped him gain much needed clarity and self-awareness. This alone time has allowed him to better understand his personality and his inner world. Through this daily practice, he is able to connect with his childhood dream of becoming an underwater adventurer. He was always fascinated toward exploring the ocean and the sea life. He has connected to his life goal and started pursuing a career as marine biologist. The time spent alone could have gone by musing and getting depressed. Rather, he utilised this time in making a concrete plan for himself and eventually connected himself with his childhood dream.

SELF-RELIANCE

Brianna, for every little decision of her life used to rely on her friends and family for advice. From managing her finances, planning her daily schedule, or even deciding on career moves, she felt more secure seeking advice from people around her rather doing it herself. This reliance made her completely dependent on others for any kind of validation. She decided to take a sabbatical from her work for self-reflection and recharge but this is an unfamiliar territory for her. She is all alone now without the daily social interactions she was used to. Without the usual support system, she felt overwhelmed, and uncertain. In simple words, this isolation was completely unsettling. But as the time passed by she accepted her solitude. She was forced to make decisions on her own now and this helped her enormously. She learned to manage her finances and keep a track of her expenses by budgeting. She used planner and time-blocking methods to architect her daily life. This self-control and self-reliance made her realise that she didn't need constant approval or guidance to make the right choices. She felt empowered and when she returned from her sabbatical, she was completely transformed. Loneliness that seemed daunting initially became an opportunity for her substantial personal growth.

EMOTIONAL HEALING

Michael has been very intelligent since childhood. Every teacher loved him, but his fellow students did not. The reason? He stutters. Wherever he went, he became the target of laughter and teasing, which badly damaged his self-image. Even though he is now grown up, his stuttering still continues. What's worse is that he has started to distance himself from his friends and relatives because of this issue. But Michael isn't going to let people laugh at him for his whole life. He has decided that enough is enough. He has promised himself that he will come back stronger and better. By using his alone time wisely, he started attending speech therapy and working through his emotions. This therapy helped him improve his communication skills and gain more confidence. With the help of a speech therapist, he practiced techniques to manage his stutter and learned strategies to navigate difficult conversations without fear and embarrassment. Slowly but surely, Michael realised that his aliment doesn't define him. With this unwavering faith he was not only able to win over his problem but also gained insight toward his life's direction. He no longer hides himself in the corner but instead steps forward with courage and engages openly in conversations. He used his loneliness creatively to become a person of eloquence and grace, transforming the pain of being alone into the peace of solitude.

ENHANCED FOCUS

Kapil stays busy at office most of the times. One meeting after the other, usual noise at workplace and fellow colleagues inviting for multiple coffee breaks. Every office goer can resonate with this type of situation. All of a sudden his organisation announced work-from-home as a part of cost cutting strategy. This transition was completely new for Kapil. He felt totally perplexed and isolated as he could not associate working officially from his home. It was also very strange to work alone without anyone to interact and chat. But, as the days went by, he saw a welcome change in his working style – his productivity was skyrocketing. Without impromptu meetings, coffee breaks, and constant interruptions, Kapil found that he could focus better on his work now. He could also structure his day better with multiple power naps and effective breaks to rejuvenate. He was able to complete multiple projects with this newly found focus and time management skill that earned him lot of accolades from his boss and promotion. This experience taught Kapil that working alone doesn't mean feeling secluded but it offers an excellent opportunity to discover self-discipline and focus that could further be translated into personal growth.

RE-EVALUATION OF RELATIONSHIPS

Who doesn't like lavish parties and huge social gatherings? An atmosphere filled with excitement, great music and scrumptious food. Well, not everyone. It all depends on individual to individual. Emma was one such person who loved being surrounded by people. She was a big party goer and was always busy on calls and chats. She never said *no* to any party plan, group chat and always stayed connected with everyone. But gradually this habit caught up to her – she started feeling exhausted and burned out. She knew her mind and body needed a break badly but her commitment didn't allow her. But one day she took a hard decision of stepping back. She started saying no to invitations, kept her phone on silent, and allowed herself quiet time. All of a sudden from lot of people around to no one around. Lot of sounds to no sound. At first, the quiet felt unsettling for her but slowly she started to enjoy the solitude. But, the biggest benefit of the decision of choosing solitude was yet to be uncovered. She started to recognise the real faces of many people. There were many who didn't even bother to call her to ask for her well-being, despite knowing she was going through a tough time. There were few relationships which were one-sided where she was the one making the effort. This realisation was a big eye-opener for her as many relationships were draining her without her noticing it. This was not easy for her to digest initially but the fact that she was able to reveal true faces of people gave her a sense of solace and empowerment. This aloneness helped her feel lighter, less overwhelmed, and far more connected to the people who really mattered.

COMPETENCY BUILDING

Ruchi finds herself deeply alone after a break-up. She has been ruminating on the moments she shared with her partner over the past decade. This has affected her deeply as she does not talk to anyone, stays all alone and at times she has been seen crying also. On suggestion of an acquaintance, she has decided to take up a skill development course. Ruchi, being a pure soul, has always been fascinated toward different cultures and diversities. She loves humanity and always ready to offer a helping hand to others without giving a second thought. So, she always wanted to learn different languages to communicate with people. But, being in a close dedicated relationship she didn't got time. But, guess what? She has ample of time now. She has enrolled herself into various language learning courses not only to enhance her domestic communication skills but global ones too. She has re-discovered her lost love of expanding her knowledge about different cultures, their people, art and history. This loneliness has proved to be a blessing in disguise for her, as it has reignited her passion and given a new life to it.

CULTIVATING PRESENT AWARENESS

David is a rich entrepreneur. His business is expanded in multiple countries. For most part of the month, he has been on travel meeting clients and visiting his regional offices. He is always accompanied by an army of officials to tend to his every need. For a long time, he is thinking to go on a solo personal trip to remote cabin in the woods. Finally, he booked one. He wanted to go away from the hustles and bustles of fast life and desired to live a simple secluded life at least for few days. All was set. He reached the destination and got everything he expected. But, he found this silence to be even more isolating and overwhelming. With no distractions and hours stretching endlessly, he found himself growing restless and lonely. One morning, while scrolling through his mobile, he stumbled upon a guide to meditation, he once saved. He immediately gave it a try. He sat on a porch, closed his eyes and focussed on his breathing. At first it was challenging for him to concentrate as he was not used to this but he practiced this daily for few days. After sometime, he noticed that his mind started to calm down. The anxiousness and restlessness was now replaced by stillness and clarity. He was now able to recognise every slightest of change around him – chirping of birds, sound of a breeze, rustling of leaves and warmth of sun. For the first time in his life, he felt complete peace inside him. His trip ended but the learning and experience lasted forever with him. He continued meditating every morning and this helped him overcome stressful moments in his life with utmost tranquillity and serenity.

What's happening here in all above real life scenarios is loneliness is acting as a *catalyst*. Initially, it surfaced to haunt, took us away from everyone, made us fearful and anxious but actually it helped us identify our real selves later on. It helped us activate our hidden potential and passion which was in sleep mode. We all could see glimpses of ours in personal growth of Robert, building of self-reliance in Brianna, Michael's emotional healing, Kapil's movement toward enhanced focus and clarity, reassessment of her social circle by Emma, Ruchi's path to competency building and David's journey into mindfulness and inner peace. To sum up, this is your chance for a fresh start—this time, enduring loneliness. Just be yourself. Be independent. Be one and have fun.

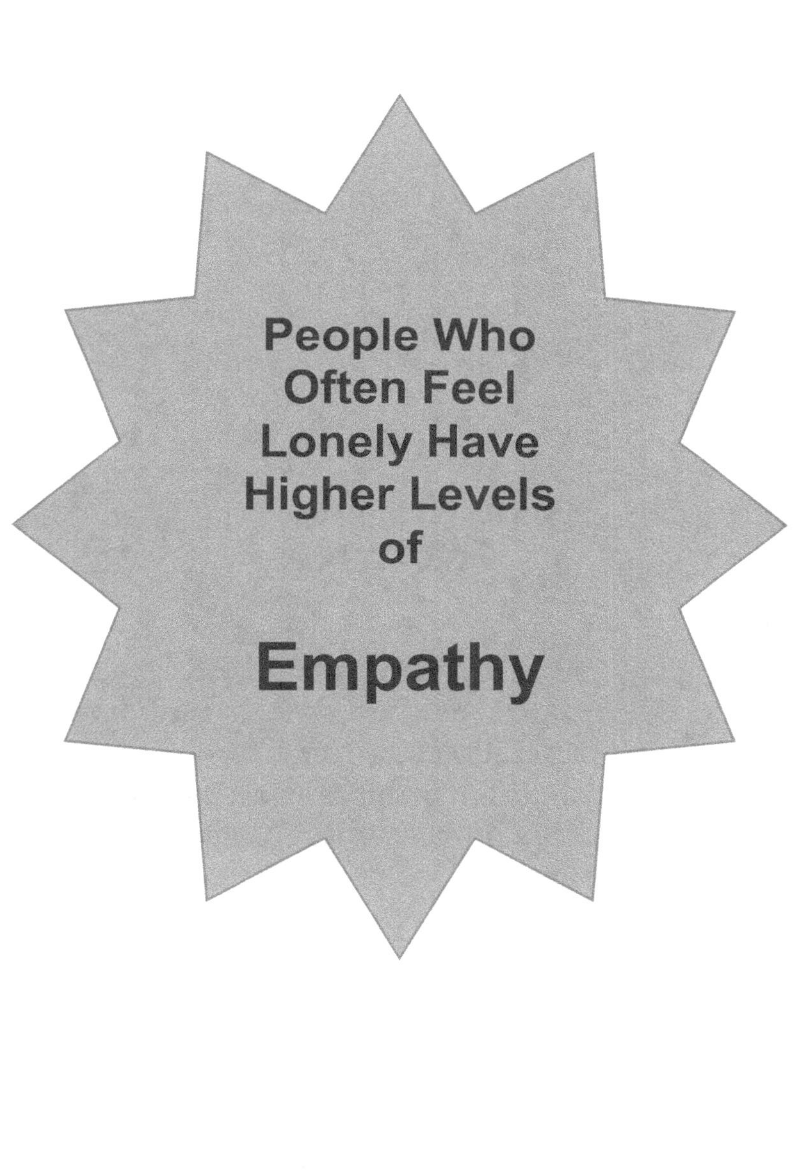People Who
Often Feel
Lonely Have
Higher Levels
of

Empathy

8.
RETURN

GOD CANNOT BE EVERYWHERE, that's why he created mother. We have heard this proverb millions of times in our lives but I would dare to change this a little bit. There are hundreds of Philanthropists, Humanitarians and Good Samaritans across the globe who had, have and are serving the humanity with their noble acts. They come from diverse backgrounds, inspired by a shared commitment to making the world a better place. Are they any less than God? Not by any logic. So, it is true that mothers offer unconditional love but generosity can never be confined to a particular gender. It's men and women both-together who god has chosen to be its stand-in. These self-less souls could be mothers, fathers, friends, mentors, strangers and countless other kind-hearted individuals who touch our lives with their love, care, and guidance, and reflect God's presence.

The reason I have chosen to start this topic on this note is to emphasize that **you, too, can become a part of this noble league of philanthropists.** Yes, you read that correctly. You can. But you must be wondering, "How can I, when I myself is struggling with loneliness?". Well, that is the divine power of God, which He has given to His representatives. Do you think all generous people are perfect and they don't have any struggles in their life? Everyone has their fair share of challenges but those who overcome these obstacles and most importantly put their lives in the service of others become *Gods-on-earth*. But the question is, how will you serve, and what will you offer? The simple answer is: your experiences and lessons from loneliness. You have come a long way. You have toiled hard. You have been betrayed by numerous. You have fought battles in silence, carrying burdens no one else could see. You have encountered setbacks that tested your resolve, yet here you stand, unshaken. People have doubted you, but you have proved them wrong with every step forward. You have learned, grown, and transformed through every trial you've faced. This is what you will offer, or in other words, this is what you will *give back*.

EVERYTHING IS NOT FOR YOU

Why does God give enormous wealth to a few when only a small amount is needed for survival? Similarly, why do some people experience more sorrows than others? It's because *everything is not for you*. This means that God chooses a few special people who can handle great wealth and bear significant pain, so they can help others on their path to prosperity. Many people go through life under the illusion that everything—success, money, or status—belongs to them. Similarly, those who face adversity often become disheartened, blaming their bad luck and misfortunes. But the real reason is something else. It's God's way of teaching and preparing us for greater tasks in life.

Oprah Winfrey grew up in poverty and faced lot of abuse in her life but this didn't deter her in becoming one of the most influential media moguls in the world. J.K. Rowling faced severe financial struggles, bouts of depression, and rejection from multiple publishers but despite these setbacks, she became one of the best-selling authors in history. Nelson Mandela spent 27 years in prison for his opposition to apartheid in South Africa but he went on to become South Africa's first black president and Nobel Peace award winner. One of the wealthiest individuals on the planet, Elon Musk once faced bullying as a child and his start-ups were on the verge of bankruptcy. Charles Dickens faced a difficult and lonely childhood, and was forced to work in a factory at a young age. He went on to become one of the greatest writers of the Victorian era. These great role models show us that before becoming famous, everyone faces enormous struggles, reminding us that at some point in their lives, everyone is humble or ordinary. It's through years of refinement, adversity, and enlightenment that they become mature enough to handle such enormous success. They had great hardships in their lives but they never cursed God for that. And, even after becoming famous they never forget God even. In both scenarios they realised that *everything is not for them*. If they have received turmoil that's because God has handpicked them as its deputies, to prepare them so that they could further teach others. And, when they became wealthy and famous they started serving humanity with their wonderful artwork and philanthropy.

Tears Help

A natural eye-cleanser. And, it cleanses the soul too. Tears are considered as signs of weakness in our society but anyone can resonate with the fact that once the emotional outpouring subsides, tears can lead to a renewed sense of self. Tears are a way of acknowledging deep emotions such as sadness, pain, or frustration that comes from feeling lonely. It's all about creating a *space* within. We have discussed this 'space' earlier in the book, and it is quite astonishing how essential it is to the process of transitioning from loneliness to solitude. How Tears help in maintaining calmness and serenity is that when these liquid droplets produced by the glands in the eyes are released, there is a space created inside. We cry when we have stuffed ourselves with so much emotion that it becomes unbearable to hold anything more. It's a natural way of relieving our body and soul from stress, overthinking, conflicts, expectations and experiences. In humble words, tears help in healing and acceptance, and this *reconciliation* is what can be returned back in the form of learnings.

Crying teaches us that the emotions need not to be suppressed. It works as a catalyst in maintaining the *flow* which can put us on the track of excellence. Crying further allows an individual to dig deep down inside and acknowledge the root cause of pain – be it loneliness, stress or any other unmet emotional need. This is how tears lead us toward the door of self-compassion and being kind to oneself while dealing with difficult emotions and vulnerability. During this process, it alleviates the weight of loneliness and let us wake up to the fact that seclusion is only a passing emotional state which can be worked through.

Most individuals cry alone – while relaxing, sleeping or walking, but we humans have an uncanny knack of detecting from eyes that the other person has just cried. Although, people love to find solace in other person's tears (as it gives them a relief that they are not the lone sufferers in this world) but it also creates a sense of sympathy among them toward that person and softens their heart. These tears somehow pull people together and assist in sustaining powerful bonds. Most significantly, this difficult situation stands out as the ultimate teacher of resilience. When we cry alone, mostly our eyes are closed and this closing of eyes helps in enduring aloneness, develop inner strength and a deeper connection with ourselves. It helps us with the understanding that this is a universal experience and everyone goes through this period of pain at least once in their lives. This epiphany serves as a profound healer and offers an unmatched coping mechanism.

POWER OF FORGIVENESS

Let me start with asking you a question.

Who do you believe people tend to resent the most?

Is it those strict teachers at school, or those friends who bully and made fun of them or those partners who betrayed them? No. It is not among those who people resent. In fact, the ones people have much anger and bitterness is toward their own parents. Yes. Quite astonishing but that's true. Some resent due to over-protection of their parents while some resent due to their neglect. Few have anger toward their parents for not able to understand them and few others have bitterness because of verbal abuse and mental & physical harassment. Many other reasons could be difference in values of child and parents, abandonment of child by parents, constant criticism and comparison with peers and siblings, favourism towards one child over other, lack of autonomy and independence and many more unmet emotional needs, unresolved conflicts and grievances. While this is true, it doesn't mean people don't love and respect their parents. Most do, and many even dedicate their entire lives to them. But, deep down inside they have that indignation also. Children crave for that unmet need from their parents which somehow will never get fulfilled.

This perhaps is one of the strongest reasons why people enmesh into the trap of loneliness. They cannot say everything to their parents and this desire remains unfulfilled inside them. This takes the shape of animosity and anger which people tend to express on their child and partners. So, the first and most important step to overcoming this negative feeling is to *forgive your parents.* I know many of you may not agree with me, but trust me, once you forgive your parents with pure intentions, you'll feel a sense of lightness and peace. This act of forgiveness will nurture the habit within you, leading to deeper peace, emotional freedom, and personal growth.

Free yourself from the cage.

Why people feel lonely is when they lock themselves in a cage and burn the bridges which could lead them out of this prison. They resent a lot from parents, siblings, friends, colleagues, neighbours and others and in doing so, they burn all the passages that could connect them with others. Only, and only power of gratitude can help them surface out of this critical situation and re-build the burned bridges. Forgiveness helps in releasing these negative feelings and can reduce the internal conflicts that often contribute to loneliness. This seclusion is not only external but out of shame or any guilt from past actions, the ill-feeling starts accumulating internally also which force many people to seclude. Self-forgiveness can heal all of these internal wounds and allow individuals to be more comfortable in their own company, thus reducing the emotional burden that fuels loneliness.

The Story of the Unforgiving Son

Once, there was a young man who lived with his father. His mother died when he was a kid. As all the responsibilities and duties came heavily on the shoulders of father, he became very strict and over critical. As a result, his son started harbouring deep resentment toward his father. As years passed, this bitterness grew even further. Son, started feeling alone and he completely avoided his father. He isolated himself not only from his father but from entire world as he didn't felt self-worth. One day, while searching something in the old wooden drawer of his father's study, he found a crumpled piece of paper which actually was a letter written by his father to him few years ago. At that time, he ignored it out of anger but this time it felt different. He opened it and his eyes spilled with tears full of compassion. In the letter, his father expressed his regret for his harsh behaviour throughout the years and asked for forgiveness. He also explained the challenges and pressures he faced to raise him as a single parent. These words struck son deeply. He realised that not only him but his father was also going through same emotional turmoil of loneliness and isolation. The anger that once burned inside him had completely faded and he decided to talk to his father. Seeing him, his father's eyes also lit up and they both embraced each other like never before. They spoke for hours, finally confronting their past hurts. This lifted the weight of resentments and regrets from both of them. Son not only connected with his father but he felt more connected with himself also. Forgiveness brought healing to him and this helped in restoring the relationship with his father, thus filling the void that loneliness had once captured.

POWER OF MENTORING

Has it ever happened that you were going somewhere and suddenly lost your way? You wandered around, searching for a way out, and then, out of nowhere, someone appeared and guided you toward a very simple and clear path? That's exactly what a *mentor* does. Someone who had been stuck in their own life and had been guided by their own mentor. Mentorship is like a chain reaction. One person mentors another, who then passes on the guidance to others, continuing the cycle. It's the passing on of experiences, lessons, and insights that one has acquired through the struggles of their own life.

How do you feel fulfilled?

Is it through success, money or position? Or is it through luxury, possessions, and the comfort of a high-status lifestyle? For years, people tend to run after materialistic things such as a lavish lifestyle, big bungalows, high-speed cars, and unlimited wealth. Yet, many still feel incomplete. They feel this way because these are just means to an end and not a completion in itself. Mentoring offers that completion. Real fulfilment is not attained through show-offs or by trying to compete and defeat others; rather, it comes from helping and making a difference in the lives of those around us. It's about teaching them what you have learnt, guiding them to walk the path of enlightenment, and sharing your experiences to empower them. Nobody teaches us this way. Since birth we have been taught to move ahead of others, compete them and defeat them. Schooling has grades to distinguish toppers and below rankers, big organisations has ranking systems to carve out profitable employees from non-profitable ones. Even in our homes, elders offer incentives to kids to go ahead of the neighbour's children. So, this is not entirely our fault. Our entire ecosystem is designed that way and we have been programmed in this fashion only. But we always have our own wisdom with us to turn this traditional way of living into something more meaningful and purposeful. By listening to our inner voice and by taking cue from our unique insights and experiences, we can transform these norms and redefine success on our own terms. If we have achieved everything in life but we don't have genuine and meaningful relationships and we are not contributing to the well-being of others, then it is not a genuine success. It's a hollow success, which is only used to create noise and there is nothing inside.

Now we know what loneliness is. We understand how it manifests. We recognize the emptiness that silence can bring. We can identify the symptoms of loneliness, and we can easily tell from the conversations, behaviours, or gestures of those around us that they are also struggling with seclusion. We will not ignore them as others have ignored us; instead, we will extend a helping hand to help them escape that cage. Whatever we have learned and understood in our journey from loneliness to solitude becomes our priority to share with others. It's a commitment to ourselves that whenever we see someone struggling with similar challenges, we will offer support and guidance. That would be a wonderful *return* and a testament to our growth. In this process of guiding and mentoring we not only surface out of our own suffering but feel even more connected to self. As we have learnt earlier also that this is a chain – a chain of actions where kindness, thoughtfulness and consideration is passed onto others. This act of giving not only enriches the receiver but also profoundly enriches the giver. It reminds us that we are never truly alone in our lives and struggles. Loneliness is always there with us to guide us, mentor us, and lead us onto the path of awakening, realisation and enlightenment.

What Next?

S O, YOU HAVE REACHED the end of yet another book. This might be your nth book of self-help but the question still lies, What next? Will you just put this book away and pick another one, or are you going to use its insights for your self-development? Loneliness was there, is there, and will always be there with you. It's forever. It's something you cannot escape or get rid of. It's a constant companion, one must learn to live with and understand rather than flee from. You can read as many books as you can about swimming, cricket or any other skill – all the strokes, hand-eye coordination or any other theoretical knowledge, but if that acquired wisdom in not applied in practical scenario then it's actually like filling up bucket full of water and never utilising it for ethical purpose. That accumulated water will soon start stagnating gradually and more water added to the bucket will either spill off or get rotten further. All in all, there will be no advantage of doing the diligent work. Similarly, if we keep reading books for knowledge but don't apply that knowledge into practicality then that knowledge will start stagnating just like still water and cannot help us in any way.

There is something amazing about fear and faith. They both are invisible but put a great ask from us of believing in them. Both are with us. In fact, within us, but which one to choose, this decision is always ours. Forever have faith in oneness. That *ONE* factor that - One more step can lead you to the right path. One change in routine can transform your entire life. One new thought can shift your entire mind-set. One decision can change your future. And, to fear, just go ahead and meet. Just one step into fear will dissipate it forever. Do new mistakes and just don't repeat the old ones. Take cue from the alone time you spent, get the learnings, be aware of the situation, be vigilant of who supports you and who betrays, but most importantly, *take action*. That is everything to combat stress, fear and loneliness. This call for action will invite fairies and angels of joy, love, peace and happiness in your life and they will stay forever with you once you keep taking regular action and get into your groove.

Loneliness is a God's signal to wake you up from the slumber and tell you that this is not the end but an opportunity to make a new beginning in your life. It is there to tell you that if you are happy inside, you will be happy from outside also. Solitude offers exceptional way to transform an isolating experience into one of profound growth and self-discovery. Just trust this divine wisdom, get fully immersed in this sea of faith and let it guide you toward peace and purpose. It's an honour to have met you and been given the chance to guide you through this transformative experience called *healing through solitude*, where loneliness becomes a pathway to deeper self-awareness and renewal.

Before you move forward and take action, I kindly ask for a small favour. If this book has resonated with you and offered valuable insights, I would greatly appreciate it if you could leave a 30-word review about this book on Amazon. Your thoughtful words could inspire and transform the lives of countless others, helping them uncover and understand the deeper meaning of loneliness. I'm here for you throughout your transformative journey, and if you have any suggestions or feedback, I would be delighted to hear from you *@rahulkapoor83@gmail.com*. It would be an honour to connect with you, listen to your story, and make a new friend. To your growth and success, cheers.

Wishing you peace, balance, and harmony.

Signing off with Love,

Rahul Kapoor

66

If you ever rejected me, disrespected me, or doubted me. Thank you.

Every time I win, I remember you.

99

ABOUT THE AUTHOR

Born in 1983, Rahul Kapoor is an emerging author from India passionate about enriching lives through positivity and creativity. With over 18 years of experience in the corporate sector, Rahul has been a catalyst for positive change, leaving a lasting impact on colleagues and peers with his cheerful demeanour and unwavering smile. Outside of work, he enjoys exploring new places, investing, and discovering healthy cuisines. Through his books, Rahul shares the invaluable insights he has gained from his journey, inspiring readers to lead more fulfilling lives.

MY JOURNEY SO FAR......

- English Books -
    1. Zero Stress
    2. Zero To One Double Zero
    3. Be A Zero, Not A Hero - Part 1
    4. Be A Zero, Not A Hero - Part 2

- Hindi Books -
    1. ज़ीरो बनिए, हीरो नहीं – भाग 1
    2. ज़ीरो बनिए, हीरो नहीं – भाग 2

PART-2
BE A ZERO, NOT A HERO
How to Build The Mindset of A Happy, Successful and Rich Person
RAHUL KAPOOR

BE A ZERO, NOT A HERO
How to Build The Mindset of A Happy, Successful and Rich Person
PART-1
RAHUL KAPOOR

खुश, सफल और अमीर व्यक्ति की मानसिकता कैसे प्राप्त करें
भाग-2
ज़ीरो बनिए, हीरो नहीं
राहुल कपूर

ज़ीरो बनिए, हीरो नहीं
खुश, सफल और अमीर व्यक्ति की मानसिकता कैसे प्राप्त करें
भाग-1
राहुल कपूर

REFERENCES

- https://en.wiktionary.org/wiki/purpose
- https://www.psychologytoday.com/us/blog/the-squeaky-wheel/201410/10-surprising-facts-about-loneliness
- https://www.bbc.com/future/article/20180928-the-surprising-truth-about-loneliness
- https://www.celebritynetworth.com/articles/billionaire-news/oprah-winfrey-escaped-a-childhood-of-poverty-and-abuse-to-become-a-billionaire-media-mogul/
- https://en.wikipedia.org/wiki/Charles_Dickens
- https://en.wikipedia.org/wiki/Elon_Musk
- https://en.wikipedia.org/wiki/J._K._Rowling
- https://en.wikipedia.org/wiki/Nelson_Mandela
- Joseph Nguyen's book, *Don't Believe Everything You Think*
- Yuval Noah Harari' book, *Sapiens: A Brief History of Humankind*

DISCLAIMER

This book is for educational purposes only. Readers acknowledge that the author does not render legal, financial, medical, or professional advice. The content within this book has been derived from various sources. Please consult a licensed professional before attempting any techniques outlined in this book.

By reading this document, the reader agrees that under no circumstances is the author responsible for any direct or indirect losses incurred as a result of the use of the information contained within this document, including but not limited to errors, omissions, or inaccuracies.

Adherence to all applicable laws and regulations, including international, federal, state, and local governing professional licensing, business practices, advertising, and all other jurisdictions, is the sole responsibility of the purchaser or reader.

Neither the author nor the publisher assumes any responsibility or liability whatsoever on behalf of the purchaser or reader of these materials. Any perceived slight of any individual or organization is purely unintentional.

9 7 9 8 3 0 2 7 2 8 7 8 4